How To Be Trustworthy

How To Be Trustworthy

KATHERINE HAWLEY

OXFORD
UNIVERSITY PRESS

OXFORD

UNIVERSITY PRESS

Great Clarendon Street, Oxford, OX2 6DP,
United Kingdom

Oxford University Press is a department of the University of Oxford.
It furthers the University's objective of excellence in research, scholarship,
and education by publishing worldwide. Oxford is a registered trade mark of
Oxford University Press in the UK and in certain other countries

First Edition published in 2019

Impression: 1

Published in the United States of America by Oxford University Press
198 Madison Avenue, New York, NY 10016, United States of America

British Library Cataloguing in Publication Data
Data available

Library of Congress Control Number: 2019937522

ISBN 978-0-19-884390-0

DOI: 10.1093/oso/9780198843900.001.0001

Printed and bound in Great Britain by
Clays Ltd, Elcograf S.p.A.

Preface

The overall aims of this book are to show that there is a core notion of trustworthiness which centrally involves avoiding unfulfilled commitments, and to explore how we face various obstacles to being trustworthy, no matter how well-meaning we are. Aiming at trustworthiness can force us into uncomfortable choices, and I show how the nature and severity of these obstacles and discomforts often depend upon our social, material, and bodily circumstances.

I have tried to write a book which will be useful—even interesting—to readers who are unfamiliar with philosophical debates about trust and trustworthiness. This includes people who are familiar with other areas of philosophy, but also people who address trust using the resources of other disciplines: I have had very fruitful cross-disciplinary conversations about trust, distrust, and trustworthiness, and hope that this book will further those engagements. Chapters 2 and 3 (about promising and asserting) are the most concerned with the nitty-gritty of philosophical debate. Whilst I have done my best to make even those chapters accessible, the book should make sense to readers who skip from chapter 1 straight to chapter 4.

In the interest of highlighting the woods rather than the trees, I have made relatively little reference to other philosophers' writings in the main body of the text, and there are neither footnotes or endnotes. But at the end of each chapter there are section-by-section indications of sources additional to those explicitly referenced in the text. These are intended to acknowledge the many ways in which I have been deeply influenced by others' writings, and to provide initial direction for those who want to explore the literature properly. I have not attempted to provide a systematic introduction to philosophical work on trust and trustworthiness, nor to the other topics I discuss. But anyone who investigates these additional sources will quickly find further guidance and route-maps.

*   *   *

A Major Research Fellowship from the Leverhulme Trust made this book both possible and necessary, and I am very grateful to the Trust for providing financial support and for embodying a humane attitude to research funding. Elements of chapters 1 and 4 are based on my 'Trust, Distrust, and Commitment', *Noûs* 48.1 (2014), 1–20, Copyright © Wiley Periodicals, Inc., permission granted by John Wiley and Sons.

I have been thinking and writing about trust—and then distrust, and then trustworthiness and untrustworthiness—for almost a decade. One of many reasons why this is a rewarding topic for research is that almost everyone is at least somewhat interested in it, and willing to chat for a while. (I have worked on other topics which don't generate the same response.) So I can't now come up with an accurate list of everyone whose comments, questions, and suggestions were influential, but I am grateful to you all. Some people have been willing to chat for more than a while, have sustained conversations over a period of years, or have provided especially important input, whether they realized it or not: these include Jessica Brown, Paul Faulkner, Sandy Goldberg, Josh Habgood-Coote, Jon Hesk, Meena Krishnamurthy, David Owens, Ishani Maitra, Onora O'Neill, and Nick Wheeler. OUP's readers all provided thoughtful, careful, useful comments, which collectively led me to reshape the book in important ways, even where I could not follow all of their suggestions. I very much appreciate the readers' investment of time and effort.

I was honoured and fortunate to be able to bookend my work on this project by giving the Mangoletsi lectures (*Distrust, Ignorance, and Injustice*) at the University of Leeds in 2010, and the Edgington lectures (*How to Be Trustworthy*) at Birkbeck, University of London, in 2018. On both occasions, the discipline of distilling my ideas into talks, followed by exceptionally thorough and constructive audience feedback, were invaluable. Along the way, I also gave talks on aspects of the project at the Universities of Aberdeen, Barcelona (LOGOS), Birmingham (Institute for Conflict, Cooperation and Security), Cambridge, Copenhagen, Durham, Edinburgh, Glasgow, Gothenburg, Graz (Women in Philosophy series), Helsinki, Liverpool, Manchester, Nottingham, Oxford, Reading, Southampton, Stirling, Toronto, Uppsala, Vienna, and York (UK); at the Institute of Education, KCL, LMU (Munich), and Trinity College Dublin; at the Irish Philosophical Club, Trust conference at Oxford's Blavatnik School of Government, Paris SOPHA conference, Madrid summer school in social epistemology, Social Epistemology Network meeting in Oslo, and an APA Pacific division panel alongside Jason D'Cruz and Karen Jones. Thanks to everyone for inviting, hosting, and cross-examining me, and to my family for tolerating all of this gadding about.

Finally, I am very grateful to my colleagues at the University of St Andrews, within and outwith Philosophy, for intellectual input, for moral support, and for providing such great raw material for this project whilst I was Head of School.

Contents

1
Trust and Distrust

Trust can be a hopeful leap in the dark; it can be the outcome of a detailed investigation. Trust can be specific to a particular task, carried out by a particular person on a particular day; it can be a generalized long-term attitude towards the people around us. Trust can make us feel warm and fuzzy; it can be the source of deep anxiety. Trust can be merited; it can turn out to have been a terrible mistake.

Trust takes on many guises, and academic researchers use many methods to study trust. Long-term opinion polls track responses to the question 'Generally speaking, would you say that most people can be trusted, or that you can't be too careful in dealing with people?' Sociologists study proxies for trust such as community involvement. Psychologists and economists design laboratory experiments measuring participants' willingness to cooperate or to take risks depending on others' cooperation; other psychologists study the effects of betrayal and trauma. Historians, political scientists, and theorists of international relations investigate how networks and attitudes of trust are built or undermined in different contexts, and between different types of agent. Organizational trust researchers study the effects of institutional culture on individual trust behaviour, and examine trust relationships between different organizations, large and small.

What can philosophers contribute to our understanding of trust? Here as elsewhere philosophers can enhance the conceptual clarity of debates, for example by distinguishing different notions of trust and its cognates, by teasing apart easily confused questions and issues, or by highlighting false dilemmas and fallacious inferences. The aim of such work is not to supplant the contributions made by other disciplines, but to offer better-honed tools for developing those contributions, and perhaps also for enabling richer contacts between different disciplines. (At the very least,

How To Be Trustworthy. Katherine Hawley, Oxford University Press (2019). © Katherine Hawley.
DOI: 10.1093/oso/9780198843900.001.0001

philosophers might enable trust researchers from other disciplines to unite against a common pernickety enemy.)

Philosophers may also hope to make a distinctive contribution to our understanding of ethical issues surrounding trust. Trust is not ethically neutral. In the right circumstances, we expect others to trust us, and it is an insult to be distrusted without good reason. Attitudes of trust and distrust carry an evaluative message, and can have far-reaching consequences of great ethical significance. Trustworthiness is an ethically admirable trait, contrasting with both dishonesty and flakiness, although this doesn't mean that being trustworthy should always be our highest ethical priority, or that there cannot be admirable reasons for dishonesty. We can discuss trust and trustworthiness without focusing on their moral dimensions, but such discussion is importantly incomplete. Philosophers are well placed to help us understand those moral dimensions, as well as to offer conceptual clarification.

1.1 Trust and Reliance

With these issues in mind, I begin in this chapter by articulating the concept of trust I will use in the rest of the book. A common core of trust is practical reliance: part of trusting people to do things is an expectation that they will in fact do those things, whilst part of trusting someone's word is relying upon what she says. Trust involves reliance. But, in the wake of Annette Baier's deservedly influential writings on trust (e.g. 1986), philosophers have generally agreed that trust involves more than mere reliance.

This distinction between trust and 'mere' reliance is motivated by considering how differently we react to misplaced trust as opposed to misplaced reliance. Suppose I trust you to look after a precious glass vase, yet you carelessly break it. I may feel betrayed and angry; recriminations will be in order; I may demand an apology. Suppose instead that I rely on a shelf to support the vase, yet the shelf collapses, breaking the vase. I will be disappointed, perhaps upset, but it would be inappropriate to feel betrayed by the shelf, or to demand an apology from it. I trusted you, but I merely relied upon the shelf. Whatever this difference amounts to, it corresponds to a difference in my reactions when things go wrong.

Inanimate objects can be relied upon without being trusted. And there are plenty of circumstances in which people are relied upon without being trusted. Suppose you regularly bring too much lunch to work, and offer the leftovers for others to eat. Suppose you do this because you're bad at judging quantities, not because you're keen to feed your colleagues. I rely on you to provide my lunch: I anticipate that you will do so, and I don't make alternative arrangements. But this reliance should not amount to trust: you would owe me no apology if you ate all the food yourself, and I ought not to feel betrayed by this, even if I felt disappointed (and hungry).

This point is often made by reference to Immanuel Kant's reputed habit of taking a walk at the exact same time every day, so reliably that people could literally set their watches by him: 'Kant's neighbors who counted on his regular habits as a clock... might be disappointed with him if he slept in one day, but not let down by him, let alone had their trust betrayed' (Baier 1986: 235). The people of Königsberg relied upon Kant for timekeeping, but sensibly did not make this a matter of trust or potential betrayal.

So there is a distinction between trust in a rich sense—trust which can be betrayed—and mere reliance. But isn't mere reliance a kind of trust too? After all, we do talk of trusting a shelf to hold a vase, or trusting a sturdy lock to keep a bike safe from thieves, even though it would be melodramatic to talk of betrayal if such things went wrong. Some philosophers have chosen to distinguish two types of trust rather than distinguishing trust from mere reliance: for example, Hollis (1998: 10) writes of 'normative' and 'predictive' trust, whilst Faulkner (2007: 880) distinguishes 'affective' from 'predictive' trust. At one level, this is a mere terminological issue: I have chosen to follow more standard philosophical usage, reserving 'trust' for the richer notion and 'mere reliance' for the other.

But a deeper question is why I and other philosophers have concerned ourselves with a distinction between trust and mere reliance which is not consistently respected by our ordinary ways of talking. The answer is that the concept of trust is central to a network of normative concepts and assessments; mere reliance does not have such rich connections. As already noted, trust, unlike mere reliance, is linked to betrayal. Moreover trustworthiness is clearly distinguished from mere reliability. Trustworthiness is admirable, something to be aspired to and inculcated in our children: it seems to be a virtue. Mere reliability, however, is not.

A reliable person is often simply predictable: someone who can be relied upon to lose keys, or to succumb to shallow rhetoric, is predictable in these respects, but isn't therefore admirable.

Even reliability in more welcome respects need not amount to trustworthiness: when you reliably bring too much lunch, you do not demonstrate trustworthiness, and nor would you demonstrate untrustworthiness if you stopped. If we mistakenly think otherwise, then we over-expand the sphere of what we can expect from other people. So the distinction between the normatively loaded attitude of trust and the merely predictive attitude of reliance is certainly significant, even if it is not tidily marked in ordinary language. Recent philosophical writing on trust has rightly taken on the challenge of explaining what this important difference consists in. The parallel distinction between distrust and lack of reliance, however, is usually overlooked.

1.2 Distrust and Non-Reliance

What is distrust? It is not a mere absence of trust. Suppose I rely upon the shelf to support the vase. This is mere reliance, falling short of the rich trust I sometimes invest in the people around me: I do not trust the shelf. But, despite this absence of trust, I do not distrust the shelf either: the features of a wooden shelf which make it an inappropriate target of trust equally make it an inappropriate target of distrust.

In fact, we can distinguish between distrust and non-reliance in much the same way as we distinguish between trust and reliance. Our reaction to misplaced trust (betrayal) differs from our reaction to misplaced reliance (disappointment). And likewise the distinction between distrust and mere non-reliance shows up in our different reactions to misplaced distrust and misplaced non-reliance. If I discover that I have wrongly distrusted you, appropriate reactions from me include remorse, apology, and requests for forgiveness. In contrast, if I take my car to be unreliable, then discover that it is after all reliable, then remorse would not be appropriate. I might regret some missed opportunities, but that's all. Not relying on an inanimate object does not amount to distrusting it.

The point extends beyond inanimate objects: not relying upon people doesn't always involve distrusting them. Sadly, my colleagues have never bought me champagne, so in particular I do not rely upon them to buy me champagne next Friday. But it would be wrong, even offensive, to say that I distrust my colleagues in this respect—after all, they have not offered to buy me champagne next Friday, and there is no social convention that they should do so. If they did buy me champagne unexpectedly, I ought to be grateful, but I would not need to feel remorse about my earlier decision not to rely on them. Indeed, it would be bad manners for me to suggest in retrospect that I should have trusted my colleagues to buy me champagne, or to apologize for my earlier non-trust.

So I do not rely upon my colleagues to buy me champagne, but this non-reliance does not amount to distrust. And rightly so, for I would be making an important mistake if I distrusted my colleagues on this basis. Not because they can after all be trusted to buy me champagne, but because neither trust nor distrust in this respect is appropriate. Earlier, I described a situation in which I relied upon you to provide enough leftovers for my lunch: this was not a matter of trust since I was entitled to feel disappointed (but not betrayed) if you stopped. Similarly, I do not rely upon my colleagues to buy me champagne, but this is not a matter of distrust, since I am not entitled to feel betrayed or angry if, as expected, they do not buy me champagne—imagine how presumptuous my feelings of resentment would be. Their 'failure' in this respect does not reflect any aspect of untrustworthiness in their characters.

Distrust is richer and more complex than mere non-reliance, just as trust is richer and more complex than mere reliance. Just as we should distinguish trustworthiness from mere reliability, we should distinguish untrustworthiness from mere unreliability: colleagues who do not buy me champagne are unreliable in this respect, but not thereby untrust-worthy. Just as there is a middle ground between trust and distrust, there is a middle ground between trustworthiness and untrustworthiness—in the clearest case, inanimate objects deserve neither trust nor distrust, so they are neither trustworthy nor untrustworthy. This is not because we do not have enough evidence to decide whether they are trustworthy or untrustworthy. It is because we know that neither of these categories apply. So 'untrustworthy'—i.e. 'meriting distrust'—is not simply the complement of 'trustworthy'. 'Distrust-worthy' would be more literal, but I will resist the neologism.

Two other linguistic glitches may have occurred to you. First, what about 'mistrust'? To my ear, and according to many dictionaries, 'distrust' and 'mistrust' are mostly interchangeable. Perhaps 'distrust' is a little more definite than 'mistrust', and perhaps it implies better justification for the attitude. But I don't think that the distinction is philosophically load-bearing, and I will stick to 'distrust'.

Second, and potentially more troubling, is that although I have been pressing a structural analogy between trust and distrust, in practice we do not treat the words 'trust' and 'distrust' symmetrically. For example, we can say that David trusts Theresa to remember his birthday, but we cannot smoothly say that Theresa distrusts David to remember her birthday. To express this thought, we might awkwardly say that Theresa distrusts David with respect to remembering her birthday. But more likely we'd just say that Theresa does not trust David to remember her birthday. That is, we attribute distrust by highlighting an absence of trust. Doesn't this conflict with my claim that distrust is an attitude in its own right, not the mere absence of trust?

I don't think so. Although there are many situations in which an absence of trust doesn't amount to distrust, there are also plenty of situations in which it's clear that either trust or distrust is appropriate, so that the absence of one indicates the presence of the other. Here's a similar phenomenon. An absence of liking doesn't amount to disliking: sometimes we feel neutral about something, sometimes we don't even know it exists. Nevertheless, there are plenty of situations in which it's clear that either liking or disliking is appropriate, so that the absence of one indicates the presence of the other. I don't like students to be late for class, which means I dislike it, but it's awkward to say that I dislike students to be late. Still, dislike is an attitude in its own right, not the mere absence of liking.

It's a nice question why English works this way, but it shouldn't distract us from more substantive issues about trust and distrust. For now, we can focus on the fact that there are plenty of situations—such as our attitudes to inanimate objects—where it is plain that trust is not appropriate, but also that distrust is not appropriate either, and not just because we are unable to make up our minds. We need to understand both trust and distrust if we are to understand the different ways in which trust can go wrong, the reasons why both trust and distrust are sometimes unwanted or unwarranted, the nature and limitations of trustworthiness, and the difference between unpredictability or unreliability and untrustworthiness.

1.3 Reliance and Non-Reliance

What about the notions of reliance and non-reliance which underlie these richer notions of trust and distrust? How are we to understand these? I adopt Richard Holton's view (1994) that to rely on someone to do something is to act on the supposition that she will do that thing. Acting on this supposition does not require an outright belief that she will do that thing, though it is incompatible with outright belief that she will not. Relying is not always a matter of belief, it can be justified by pragmatic reasons (e.g. convenience or politeness) as well as or instead of reasons which point towards the truth of the supposition that the person will act that way. Moreover, unlike believing, relying is sometimes a matter of direct choice.

In this sense, relying on someone to do something needn't mean putting your fate in their hands. You can rely upon me to bring enough food for everyone at the picnic whilst nevertheless bringing plenty of food yourself, because you don't want to seem ungenerous: you're acting on the supposition that I will bring lots of food, and indeed this partly explains the large quantities you bring along. Thus reliance in this sense needn't imply substantial risk or genuine vulnerability. Building an account of trust on this notion of reliability therefore leaves space for cases in which someone trusts another without taking any significant risks, and without making herself vulnerable through her trust.

For me, this is one attraction of Holton's account: it allows us to investigate when and why trust can make us (more) vulnerable, without writing vulnerability into the very definition of trust. But others will prefer a more demanding account of reliance and therefore trust, in order to focus on what seem like the most significant cases. We can all agree that the decision whether to rely on someone takes on special importance when reliance brings vulnerability; circumstances in which one cannot avoid vulnerability are of distinctive interest; moreover our duties to be trustworthy seem to be heightened when others are vulnerable to us.

I recognize all of these points, and will return to some of them later in this book. But for now my strategy is to offer an account of trust and trustworthiness quite generally, rather than focusing on situations of greater vulnerability.

So relying on someone to do something involves presupposing that she will act as expected. And trust involves such reliance, plus some further factor we have not yet explored. What about distrust and non-reliance? Although trust involves confident prediction of appropriate behaviour, distrust does not require confident prediction of misbehaviour. So distrusting someone with respect to a certain act involves not relying upon her to act that way, rather than relying upon her *not* to act that way. Extending Holton's framework, non-reliance means not acting on a particular positive supposition, rather than acting on the corresponding negative supposition.

There are good questions to ask about degrees of reliance, degrees of reliability, and the fact that suppositions are sometimes idle wheels. When I don't need your help, it may make no practical difference whether or not I act under the supposition that you would help if asked.

It's also not clear what to say about situations in which I outwardly act as if I suppose that you will do something, yet inwardly fret that you will not: is this reliance? Disagreements on this point may reflect broader disagreements about what trust feels like. Some picture trust as a kind of relaxed confidence, incompatible with inner fretting. On a different picture, we sometimes trust—or are left with no option but to trust—despite our doubts, and without thereby erasing those doubts. I am inclined towards the second of these pictures, so that trust and reliance are both compatible with anxiety. But overall I do not have anything particularly insightful to say about borderline cases of reliance: I am consoled by the fact that similar questions arise for many, perhaps all, different accounts of trust. Moreover, our understanding of these grey areas between reliance and non-reliance can only be enhanced by paying proper attention to distrust alongside trust, as I recommend.

1.4 The Commitment Account

So how can we best understand both the difference between trust and mere reliance, and the difference between distrust and non-reliance?

In my view, the notion of commitment is key, and the commitments I have in mind are those which generate obligations whether we like it or not. I will explain the commitment account of trust and distrust, and some of its strengths, before discussing its limitations, and why others have preferred alternative accounts. I do not think that this view can capture absolutely everything which gets called 'trust' or 'distrust'. Nor can it satisfactorily account for all the phenomena which draw people from many academic disciplines to the study of trust. But I will argue that it does capture a central and ethically significant notion of trust (and of distrust), one which connects in fruitful ways to other important notions; some of these connections will be drawn out later in the book.

So: recall the situation in which you reliably bring too much lunch to work, because you are a bad judge of quantities, and I get to eat your leftovers. My attitude to you in this situation is one of reliance, but not trust, and your reliability in this respect shows nothing about whether you are trustworthy. In my view, this is not a matter of trust—or distrust— because you have made no commitment to provide me with lunch. But if we adapt the case so as to suggest commitment, it starts to look more like a matter of trust. Suppose we enjoy eating together regularly, you describe your plans for the next day, I say how much I'm looking forward to it, and so on. To the extent that this involves a commitment on your part, it seems reasonable for me to feel betrayed and expect apologies if one day you fail to bring lunch and I go hungry.

Recognized lack of commitment also explains our judgement about the colleagues who do not buy me champagne. They are unreliable in this respect, but it would be unreasonable of me therefore to distrust them, or to consider them untrustworthy in any respect. They have not offered to buy me champagne, and there's no social convention that they should do so. They have incurred no commitment to buy me champagne and so their failure to do so is not a failure of trustworthiness.

Here is my account of trust and distrust:

- To trust someone to do something is to believe that she has a commitment to doing it, and to rely upon her to meet that commitment.

- To distrust someone to do something is to believe that she has a commitment to doing it, and yet not rely upon her to meet that commitment.

(If you cannot accept the formulation 'distrust someone to do something', then I hope that you can get along with 'distrust someone in respect of doing something', at least for long enough to see why I think that the benefits of this account outweigh the awkwardness of this formulation.)

The central notion of commitment needs immediate clarification. In one sense, having a commitment to do something involves having a determined intention to do it; this is the sense in which we can admire someone's commitment to a project. But, crucially, this is not the relevant sense for the commitment account of trust and distrust. After all, this sort of psychological commitment is often exactly what's missing when distrust is appropriate.

In the relevant sense, one can be committed to doing something one has no intention of doing: if I've promised to come to your birthday party, but I now decide I can't be bothered, I still have a commitment in the relevant sense, even though I have no intention of fulfilling it. This is of course a situation which makes distrust appropriate: I undertook to do something but don't intend to live up to my commitment, and if you know this about me, then you should distrust me in this respect at least.

Promising is one clear, even paradigmatic way of acquiring the relevant sort of commitment; I explore promising in some depth in chapter 2. But explicit promising is not the only route to commitment; if it were I would be able to account for only a narrow range of cases of trust and distrust. After all, there seem to be obvious, immediate counterexamples to the claim that trust and distrust presuppose that commitment has been incurred through explicit promise-making. We often trust people to do things which we know they have not explicitly promised to do. I trust my friends not to steal my books when they come to my house, and, at least in some circumstances, I trust strangers to let me walk unhindered. Indeed, an important element of trust involves trusting people not to be overly legalistic about what they are committed to doing. Sticking to the letter of a promise rather than its spirit can often be a form of untrustworthiness: think of election pledges.

So to make my account plausible I must use a very broad notion of commitment: commitments can be implicit or explicit, weighty or trivial, conferred by roles and external circumstances, default or acquired, welcome or unwelcome. In particular I will take it that mutual expectation and convention give rise to commitment unless we take steps to disown these. In chapter 3 I will argue that assertion or telling involves commitment, so that trusting someone's word falls within the scope of the account.

Although I hope that this notion will become clearer as I use it, I do not offer anything like an analysis or a reductive account of commitment. But this doesn't meant that my account of trust and distrust can be gerrymandered to fit just any old judgement about cases. Although there are borderline cases, there are also clear cases of commitment, and of non-commitment, and these are, respectively, cases in which either trust or distrust is appropriate, and cases in which neither trust or distrust is appropriate. Indeed, we will come across cases where the right verdict seems to be that it is indeterminate whether commitment has been incurred, and that it is therefore indeterminate whether either trust or distrust is appropriate. In section 5.1 I explore the ways in which we can lack insight into our own commitments, and even lack control over which commitments we are landed with. For now, I will primarily focus upon transparent, voluntary commitments, but that is not intended to be the full picture.

I think it is clear that there is an important attitude we bear to other people when we rely upon them to live up to their commitments; this much should be acceptable even to those who hesitate to call this attitude 'trust'. I plan to explore this attitude, and, relatedly, to investigate the demands and significance of living up to one's commitments. It is often unclear whether someone has incurred a commitment in the relevant sense. But this is a real-life characteristic of social interaction, and the source of distinctive kinds of difficulties; these unclarities should be recognized by our theorizing, not defined out of existence.

Should we instead place obligation rather than commitment at the heart of trust and distrust? Commitments typically give us obligations; and perhaps I have stretched the notion of commitment far enough to ensure that obligations always give us commitments. Perhaps trusting someone to do something is a matter of thinking her obliged to do it, and relying upon her to fulfil her obligation, whilst distrusting involves taking someone to have an obligation, yet not relying upon her to fulfil it.

This seems nearly right. But such an account washes out the distinctiveness of trust, distrust, trustworthiness, and untrustworthiness. For example, the virtue of being trustworthy is not the very general virtue of meeting one's obligations. Relatedly, being trustworthy does not involve meeting all legitimate expectations, only those legitimate expectations which are distinctively associated with trust and distrust. In fact, the way in which trustworthiness requires less than all-round good behaviour is the source of some of the most interesting difficulties and tensions we encounter around trustworthiness; I explore these in more depth in chapter 4, and follow their consequences through chapters 5 and 6.

Another question about commitment: when I trust-or-distrust some-one, must I believe that she has a commitment *to me*? Or is it enough that I believe that she has a commitment to someone or other? I will take it that trust-or-distrust requires only that we think the person has a commitment to someone or other. For example, suppose your daughter's friend promises to her (not to you) that she will stay to the end of the party and give your daughter a lift home. Suppose you rely upon the friend to keep this promise: you drink several glasses of wine, making it impossible for you to safely drive and fetch your daughter yourself. I will take it that you trust your daughter's friend to keep her promise to your daughter.

But if this seems implausible, then the commitment account could in principle be restricted so that genuine trust-or-distrust is available only when we think someone has made a commitment to us. We might then say that you judge your daughter's friend to be trustworthy in this respect, and that you believe it's appropriate for your daughter to trust her, but that strictly speaking you can neither trust nor distrust her yourself, since she made no promise to you. This restriction coheres with accounts of trust which emphasize its second-personal character; I will return to the issue when I discuss betrayal in section 1.7.

Relatedly, we may wonder whether a person can make a commitment to herself, and thus underpin self-trust, or indeed self-distrust. In the psychological sense of commitment, a person can have a determined intention to do something for her own sake. But this is not the sense of commitment I have invoked to understand trust and distrust—i.e. commitment of the kind which can be generated through promising. Although we talk of making promises to ourselves, there seems to be an important difference between such cases and promises to others, from which we cannot unilaterally release ourselves. More generally, self-trust seems a poor fit for the issues which preoccupy me later in this book, which turn on the social costs and benefits of trustworthiness.

1.5 Looking Beyond Expectations

As I have presented it so far, the commitment account is a primarily an account of trust, and of distrust—i.e. of our attitudes towards others. But, as I have hinted, one of its key strengths is that it readily corresponds to a substantive account of what trustworthiness and untrustworthiness amount to. Given that trust aims at trustworthiness—as a rule, we try to ensure that our trust is mostly directed at trustworthy people—this gives us an account of what makes trust accurate or inaccurate. Likewise for distrust. Perhaps surprisingly, not every account of the nature of trust provides us with insight into the nature of trustworthiness. To illustrate this, I will now discuss the views of Richard Holton (1994) and of Karen Jones (2004); these are not antithetical to my own, but they illustrate how accounts of trust do not automatically illuminate trustworthiness.

Holton invokes the 'participant stance', an attitude of treating others as people in their own right, not as mere features of the world:

> I think that the difference between trust and [mere] reliance is that trust involves something like a participant stance towards the person you are trusting...trusting someone is one way of treating them as a person. But if this is right, it shows how important it is that we do not treat the participant stance as an all or nothing affair. Even when you do trust a person, you need not trust them in every way....You can trust a person to do some things without trusting them to do others.
>
> (Holton 1994: 4)

Taking the participant stance towards someone does seem to be a necessary condition for trust, since it makes reactive attitudes possible. Indeed, following Baier (1986) I earlier identified trust via its connections with reactive attitudes such as resentment and the sense of betrayal. Moreover taking the participant stance seems also to be a necessary condition for distrust: we do not distrust faulty machines, or wonky shelves. So there is clearly something right about this approach. But the trouble is that interpersonal respect for others sometimes requires us neither to trust nor to distrust them in a given regard, since to do so would be an imposition.

Suppose that my colleagues do after all plan to buy me champagne. Still, they do not invite or welcome my trust in this respect; instead, they want to give me a treat, not merely to act as trustworthiness requires, and certainly not to risk betraying me if they forget to buy the champagne, or realize they can't afford it. Similar situations arise in even the most intimate, trusting relationships. Imagine that I cook dinner for my husband each evening and he comes to rely on this. Even if I enjoy cooking, in this scenario I do not want my husband to make this a matter of trust. That is, I do not want to risk betraying him in even a minor way if I don't cook one evening, and nor do I want that to count against my trustworthiness. We aspire to a completely trusting relationship—we would like to avoid even the slightest distrust—but we do not aspire to turn all our interactions into issues of trust, for that would be oppressively exhausting. (What if we disagree about whether a particular issue or interaction should be an issue of trust? I will take up such thorny issues in chapters 5 and 6.)

Holton correctly identifies the participant stance as a necessary element of trust, and adopting this stance is necessary for distrust too. But relying upon someone to whom you take a participant stance does not always mean trusting that person: some interactions lie outside the realm of trust and distrust. Likewise, deciding not to rely upon someone to whom you take a participant stance need not mean distrusting that person: you may just decide to buy your own champagne, or give up any aspiration to drinking champagne. And adopting the participant stance can sometimes require us not to turn every interaction into a matter of trust and distrust. But such non-trust interactions are still within the scope of the participant stance: it's supremely appropriate for my husband to express his gratitude for my cooking, even though he should not convert his reliance into trust.

Jones (2004) also connects trust and the reactive attitudes but in a more modulated fashion than Holton:

> [Three-place t]rust is accepted vulnerability to another person's power over something one cares about, where (1) the truster foregoes searching (at the time) for ways to reduce such vulnerability, and (2) the truster maintains normative expectations of the one-trusted that they not use that power to harm what is entrusted.   (2004: 6)

For my present purposes, I will take it that the notions of accepted vulnerability plus forgoing the attempt to reduce such vulnerability capture roughly the notion of reliance. One might have something a bit like this attitude to an inanimate object like a car, for example. Only 'a bit like', because there are crucial differences between Jones's notion, character- ized in terms of power, care, vulnerability, and harm, and the thinner characterization of reliance I have adopted from Holton. But, as I said earlier, once we have framed an account of trust and trustworthiness in rather thin terms, we can go on to identify certain situations—perhaps exactly those in which there is vulnerability and risk—as being of special moral significance.

In this context, normative expectations must do the work of distin- guishing trust from mere reliance. Normative expectations, for Jones, are 'multistranded dispositions, including dispositions to evaluative judgement and to reactive attitudes' (2004: 17, note 8): when you trust someone, you are liable to feel resentful if she lets you down through ill will or laziness, and whilst you might not feel resentful if she lets you down by accident, you may still think that an apology is warranted. Jones distinguishes normative expectations from predictive expectations: we can normatively expect something of someone without predicting that she will in fact do what we expect of her.

If this is trust, what might distrust be? Let's understand non-reliance as a refusal to accept vulnerability, or as a continuing attempt to reduce such vulnerability. One might have this attitude to a machine one takes to be unreliable. What more is needed for distrust? Plausibly, the norma- tive expectations involved in distrust are exactly the normative expect- ations which would otherwise be involved in trusting that person in that respect. So distrust is non-reliance plus a tendency to resentment, a tendency to judge the distrustee negatively, or tendency to think that an apology is warranted: distrust is something like disappointed trust, though perhaps not preceded by an episode of trust.

Because Jones pins normative expectations to specific tasks (or, rather, to specific cared-for things), she can accommodate the important fact that respect for others, even in very intimate relationships, can require us to stick with reliance-or-non-reliance rather than trust-or-distrust in certain respects. I am happy for my husband to predict that I will cook dinner tonight, but I do not want him to develop normative expect- ations, to be poised to resent me if I don't cook.

Normative expectations can help us understand both trust and dis- trust, but there is something important missing from the picture. Both

Holton and Jones tell us more about the truster's attitudes than they do about the features of the trustee to which those attitudes are directed. We also need a story about when trust, distrust, or neither is objectively appropriate—what is the worldly situation to which (dis)trust is an appropriate response? When is it appropriate to have (dis)trust-related normative expectations of someone? This is not just a question of practical self-interest or mental hygiene: we owe it to others to get this right. Mistaken distrust can be insulting, and limit other people's options, Mistaken trust can be burdensome, or allow vulnerable others more leeway than they can properly manage.

We also need to understand the virtue of trustworthiness and the vice of untrustworthiness, as they are distinguished from reliability and unreliability. To do all this, we need a basis for our judgements about reliability: how, if at all, can we predict what others will do? (A closely related question is key to the epistemology of testimony: how, if at all, can we judge who is speaking truthfully?) But we also need a basis for our judgements about when it is appropriate to trust-or-distrust, not merely to rely-or-not-rely. Many of the relevant norms apply only when we enter the realm of appropriate trust-or-distrust.

The commitment account of trust and distrust provides this extra richness. Seeing others as having undertaken commitments to us engages the participant stance; it makes us poised for certain distinctive reactive attitudes, specifically resentment when commitments are not met, and a measure of regret about earlier distrust when commitments are unexpectedly fulfilled. It also allow us to distinguish between situations in which trust is inappropriate because the person in question is not reliable, and situations in which trust is inappropriate because the person does not in fact have the relevant commitment.

1.6 Why Commitment Rather than Motives?

Like most other philosophers writing in this tradition, I am taking trust to involve reliance, plus some extra factor. Unlike many other philosophers, I have not identified this extra factor with a positive view of the motives of the trusted person. A motives-based account has it that if I trust you to look after my vase then I rely upon you to do so, and moreover I take it that you have the right kind of motive for looking after my vase; different accounts disagree about what the 'right kind' of motive might be, but typically this will involve some sort of concern for me.

Motives-based accounts seem initially to be a good fit for the distinction between trust and mere reliance: after all, when I merely rely upon the shelf to hold the vase I don't impute any kind of motive to the shelf, and when I merely rely upon you to generate leftovers for my lunch I know that you do not do this with my interests in mind. Moreover, motives-based accounts seem to offer a more illuminating account of trustworthiness: it will involve acting out of the right kind of motives.

But the emphasis on motives seems less attractive when we attempt to extend the picture to include distrust. I cannot survey every motives-based account of trust but will focus on representative suggestions from Russell Hardin (2002) and Karen Jones (1996) (this view differs from Jones's 2004 account, which as we saw above is framed in terms of normative expectations). Both theories are well developed, sophisticated, and prominent in the literature. Moreover they differ significantly from one another, turning on the trustee's rational self-interest and other-directed goodwill respectively.

Hardin argues that when we trust someone, we expect the trustee to encapsulate our interests within her own, because she has an interest in maintaining or strengthening her relationship with us. In trusting you to look after my vase, I take it that you will do so because you have incorporated my interest in preserving the vase amongst your own interests: looking after the vase now serves your own interests. In contrast, when I rely upon the shelf to hold the vase, I do not have any expectation about the shelf's motives or interests, for I realize it has none.

Jones defines trust as an attitude of optimism that the goodwill and competence of another will extend to cover the domain of our interaction with her, together with the expectation that the one trusted will be directly and favourably moved by the thought that we are counting on her (1996: 1). As with Hardin, it is clear how this definition entails that we do not trust the shelf when we rely upon it to hold the vase. Moreover reference to the trustee's responsiveness to our counting on her permits a distinction between genuine trustworthiness and reliable but paternalistic benevolence.

Hardin and Jones have each identified genuine attitudes that we do indeed sometimes adopt to one another. Moreover these attitudes may sometimes be of great significance to all concerned. But if we identify either of these attitudes with trust, we limit our ability to account for a wide range of related phenomena, including distrust and trustworthiness. On the motives-based picture, we might expect distrust to involve non-reliance, plus a negative attitude regarding the motives of the person distrusted.

This negative attitude must go beyond expecting the person to lack the motives required for trustworthiness. After all, inanimate objects lack the motives required for trustworthiness: they do not incorporate our interests amongst their own, and they do not act out of goodwill towards us. Yet we do not distrust inanimate objects, even when we decide not to rely upon them. The same is often true in interpersonal situations. Consider the colleagues who do not buy me champagne. I do not rely upon them to buy me champagne; moreover I know that they have not incorporated my interest in drinking champagne amongst their own interests, and sadly I am not optimistic about their goodwill in the champagne-buying domain. Yet it's not appropriate for me to distrust my colleagues: they are not displaying untrustworthiness, and if they do surprise me with champagne I needn't feel remorse about not having trusted them. Neither trust nor distrust is appropriate in this context.

So if distrust involves an imputation of motives, these must be more sinister than the mere absence of positive motives towards us. Perhaps distrust involves expectation that the person will act out of ill will towards us, or to have an interest in frustrating our interests. This would explain why we do not distrust inanimate objects (contrary to occasional appearances, they are not actively working against us), and why I should not distrust my colleagues (they are not maliciously striving to deny me champagne).

But neither expectation of ill will nor expectation of attempts to frustrate my interests is necessary for distrust. After all, someone who lies and cheats to achieve her goals should be distrusted, even if she does not bother to bear either goodwill or ill will to others, and does not care about other people's interests. Nor are gloomy expectations sufficient for distrust, even in combination with non-reliance. Suppose that a deeply honourable person campaigns to have me imprisoned for my real and heinous crimes. I cannot rely on this person to help me; moreover I know that she bears me ill-will and is actively trying to frustrate my goals. But my attitude to her needn't amount to distrust, for she is straightforward and honest in her campaigning. (This doesn't mean that I should trust her; only that I do not have grounds to distrust her.) My opponent does not display untrustworthiness in her open campaigning against me. And if she turns out to be more helpful than I had expected, I need not feel remorse about my previous attitude of non-reliance.

Now, I have not explored all the options here, nor represented the full complexity of Hardin's and Jones's positions. Nevertheless, I have shown that neither account of trust can handle distrust easily, and this for reasons which generalize to other motives-based accounts. Both Hardin and Jones take care to distinguish genuine trust from mere reliance. But each considers decisions about distrust only in situations where either genuine trust or genuine distrust is appropriate, where a person's behaviour demonstrates either trustworthiness or untrustworthiness (i.e. distrust-worthiness). This narrow focus means that trust, distrust, and indecision seem to exhaust the options, leading Hardin and Jones to think of distrust as a kind of decisive lack of trust (Hardin 2002: 90; Jones 1996: 17; see also McLeod 2002: 34).

Instead, we should ask about the preconditions for trust-or-distrust: what is it about the excess-lunch-bringer, the non-champagne-buyers, and indeed inanimate objects which mean that they are not suitable recipients of either trust or distrust in the relevant respects? The primary reason that trust is not appropriate in these cases is that neither trust or distrust is appropriate. And—in my view—this is because there is no commitment involved, not because of any feature of the other person's motives or interests.

Might we understand trust in terms of both commitment and motive? The idea might be that when I trust someone I take her to have a commitment, and I take her to be motivated by that commitment in ways which make her reliable. Correspondingly, perhaps when I distrust someone I take her to have a commitment, yet take her to be insufficiently motivated by that commitment, so that I do not rely upon her. I reject these suggestions, for reasons that I will explain more fully later: I will return to the relationship between trustworthiness and being motivated by commitment in section 4.1, and I comment again on the (un)importance of motive in section 1.8. In my view good motives are neither necessary nor sufficient for trustworthy action, and thus they are neither necessary nor sufficient for appropriate trust.

1.7 Betrayal

Getting it right about reliance is important. If someone relies upon a rope bridge to hold their weight, but the bridge is unreliable, the practical consequences might be very serious, even unto death. If someone relies upon Kant's regular morning walk as a reminder to take their medication, but Kant is unreliable in this respect, this might also lead to the ultimate bad consequence. Relying on the unreliable can be dangerous.

But trusting the untrustworthy can generate harms go beyond those caused by relying on the unreliable. One sort of harm is emotional damage caused by discovering that you have trusted someone who turned out not to deserve your trust. This sort of damage can have long-ranging and complex consequences. Important though such harms are, I will set them aside here in order to discuss the kind of distinctive harm done when trust is violated, even if the violation is never discovered and so does not cause emotional damage.

It does seem that there is something intrinsically problematic about betrayals or violations of trust, something in addition to both the practical consequences of unreliability and the emotional consequences of discovering such violations: the wrong of lying, cheating, and promise-breaking goes beyond its contingent practical harm. But being trusted is neither a necessary nor a sufficient condition for the possibility of such betrayal.

Trust is not necessary, because we can be betrayed by those we distrust, and indeed distrust can include expectation of betrayal. You can know that you will be betrayed: Jesus knew that Judas would betray him. Yet trust is incompatible with outright belief that betrayal will occur, so betrayal does not require trust. Relatedly, if I lie to you and you are not misled, the practical damage may be mitigated, yet I wrong you nonetheless, and not just through any emotional damage I may cause. Finally, if you trust me and I prove untrustworthy, my behaviour does not become acceptable once your trust ceases. In such cases, there may be practical consequences of unreliability, or emotional consequences of the discovery of untrustworthiness. But, on the assumption that there is a further, intrinsic wrongness in violating trust, there is likewise a further, intrinsic wrongness in being untrustworthy even when you are not trusted.

Conversely, we do not always do wrong when we knowingly disappoint those who trust us. We can distinguish two kinds of mistake in trusting: trusting someone who merits distrust, and trusting someone in a respect which merits only reliance or non-reliance. The first of these involves recognizing that someone is a suitable target for our normative expectations, but misjudging their reliability: this kind of mistake results in betrayal. But the second is a mistake about whether someone is a suitable target for normative expectations in this respect: if such a person proves unreliable, we may feel betrayed, but we have not been betrayed, and the trustee may rightly complain of our moralizing presumption.

The commitment account can explain all this: we do wrong when we fail to fulfil a commitment, absent mitigating circumstances. This is independent of whether we are in fact expected to fulfil the commitment—i.e. whether we are trusted or distrusted in this respect. Being trusted is not necessary. Moreover, if someone mistakenly thinks I have a commitment, and I do not act as that supposed commitment would require, then I have not in fact behaved badly. Letting down someone who trusts is not sufficient for morally problematic violation of trust, regrettable though it may often be.

Granted, in some circumstances we acquire commitments simply by allowing others to continue to rely upon us, or by allowing others to think that we have commitments. And we cannot always minimize commitment and thus minimize the risk of unmet commitments: this fetishization of honour would in any case make for an unrewarding, lonely life. Nevertheless, we are not entirely at the mercy of others' decisions to trust us.

I argued above that trust-or-distrust does not require a direct relationship: you trust your daughter's friend to keep her promise to your daughter, even though the friend has made no commitment to you. But are you really betrayed when someone fails to meet a commitment to a third party? It seems more plausible to say that the only person betrayed is the person to whom the commitment is made. This weakens, though does not break, the connection between trust and betrayal. The alternative is to rule that genuine trust-or-distrust is available only to those to whom commitments are made.

This uneasy dilemma is not generated by the commitment account per se; rather, it arises from a tension between two tempting thoughts about cases like that of your daughter's friend. On the one hand, it is natural to think of your attitude towards your daughter's friend as trust: you are disposed to hold many of the trust-related reactive attitudes towards your daughter's friend, and reasonably so. On the other hand, it is natural to think that it is only your daughter who is betrayed if her friend breaks her promise to her. Any account of trust (and distrust) must make a difficult choice between retaining these two intuitive judgements whilst weakening the trust–betrayal connection, or else retaining the trust–betrayal connection whilst rejecting one of the two intuitions.

Motives-based accounts of trust treat distrust as an afterthought and thus struggle to explain the wrong involved in violating trust. On such accounts, to trust someone to do something is to rely upon her to do it for the right sort of motives. Such trust is disappointed either when the task is not completed or else when the motives are 'wrong'. This makes unfeasibly heavy demands upon trustees, putting us in moral jeopardy, liable to betray—not just disappoint—people who have unrealistic expectations of us. My colleagues don't care about my interest in drinking champagne, nor do they bear me goodwill in this respect; surely they cannot be criticized for this. But if I foolishly persuade myself otherwise, then on such accounts my colleagues will subsequently 'betray' me when they fail to buy champagne.

Moreover understanding trust (and distrust) in terms of normative expectations does not by itself explain when such expectations are appropriate. If I unreasonably develop normative expectations of my colleagues in respect of champagne-buying—whether or not I also pre-dict that they will buy me champagne—then I will wrongly feel betrayed when they do not buy me champagne.

Now, we do indeed sometimes develop inappropriate expectations of one another, and end up feeling resentful or betrayed. But the commit-ment account enables us to see this as a consequence of miscommu-nication or misunderstanding about what commitments have been undertaken, rather than inevitably casting the fault upon the person who 'fails' to act as expected. In chapters 5 and 6 I will discuss the ways in which such miscommunication can arise, and how it can be avoided.

[handwritten margin note, left: But other commitments are than trust commitment]

1.8 Where Next?

[handwritten margin note, right: I'm not sure I agree with this — it takes an absolute value of trust]

When we think about trust, we wonder who merits our trust, why, and to what degree. When we think about trustworthiness, we are anchored by the obvious thought that to be trustworthy is to merit trust. So trust and trustworthiness are enmeshed. My own view is that trustworthiness is best understood in terms of commitment—to be trustworthy is to live up to one's commitments, whilst to be untrustworthy is to fail to live up to one's commitments—and correspondingly that the attitude of trust involves expectations of commitment-fulfilment. Understanding trust in terms of seeing commitment in others enables us to understand the differences between distrust, suspension of judgement between trust and distrust, and cases where we clearly judge that neither trust nor distrust is appropriate. Moreover it gives us a grasp of what trust aims at, of what trustworthiness requires: matching commitment with action.

Let me concede before going any further that this account does not make sense of every ordinary use of the word 'trust'. Nor does it capture everything that theorists have wanted from an account of trust. I have already noted that there is a more demanding notion of trust which ties it more closely to risk and vulnerability: I don't deny that trust takes on special significance in such contexts, but I see these as special instances of a more general attitude of trust.

In addition, I am not placing much weight on people's motives for living up to their commitments, or failing to do so. On my view, if someone lives up to her commitments for purely mercenary reasons (to earn her salary, to bank favours, to avoid punishment), or for the self-aggrandizing pleasure of placing herself on a moral pedestal, this in itself does not undermine her trustworthiness. But of course there are morally significant differences between someone like this, and someone who lives up to her commitments for more noble reasons, perhaps involving her sense of honour, or indeed others' dependence upon her. And often when we trust someone we hope and expect that she will live up to her commitments for more admirable reasons, and we may feel disappointed if baser motives are in play. This emphasis on the 'right' motives may be especially common within intimate personal relationships. In the workplace, on the other hand, motives may seem less important so long as things get done. Our attitudes to politicians and public figures seem to waver between these poles.

Are you tempted to insist that only such nobility constitutes genuine trustworthiness, unlike the superficial patterns of seemingly trustworthy behaviour I am prepared to dignify with the term? Then let's not quarrel over terminology. I will argue that commitment-fulfilment (or its absence) is important and interesting in all sorts of ways, regardless of motive, but I will not insist that this is the only important or interesting notion in the vicinity. I will continue to use the language of trustworthiness in discussing this habit of commitment-fulfilment, but if you wish to substitute a less grand label, you are welcome to do so.

Another potential concern: the attitude of trust which corresponds to this commitment-based notion of trustworthiness has no distinctive phenomenology, since it is at heart merely an expectation regarding another's behaviour under certain circumstances. One can trust without experiencing any particular feeling or emotion, on this view. But of course trust (and distrust) can have enormous emotional significance, especially in the context of personal relationships. Again, if you are tempted to insist that it's not really trust if it doesn't have the appropriate emotional texture, then we may not have a deep-seated disagreement. I will argue that the attitude I call 'trust' is interesting and important in lots of ways, but this is not to diminish the significance of more phenomenologically distinctive attitudes.

Rival notions are often special cases of the more general notion I call 'trust', or 'trustworthiness'. Well-motivated commitment-fulfilment is a type of commitment-fulfilment more generally, and emotionally charged expectations of commitment-fulfilment are nevertheless expectations of commitment-fulfilment. But are there plausible rival notions of trust or trustworthiness that do not fit this pattern? Here I will put up more resistance: I think we do need to see commitment as central to the concepts of trust and trustworthiness in order to understand many of the ways in which we use those concepts, and moreover to understand the relatively neglected notions of distrust and untrustworthiness. Nevertheless, there are of course important and valuable traits, virtues, and patterns of behaviour which correspond to a habit of responding to others' needs and wishes, whether or not one is committed to doing so. My main point is that it is useful to separate these things conceptually: I will explore this in greater depth in chapter 4.

Finally, let me acknowledge that I am focusing on trust as a three-place relation, involving two people and a task: you may trust me to look after your children, to keep a secret, or to tell the truth. We do however sometimes speak of simply trusting someone, and I will return to this notion of generalized trust and the corresponding notion of trustworthiness in chapter 4.

In the next two chapters I will explore first promising and then telling, treating both as the explicit acquisition of commitment. Indeed I will argue that telling is a type of promising. My particular concern will be the norms which govern promising, and thus telling. Promises should be sincere, but in addition there are competence norms on promise-making: we shouldn't make promises we are not well placed to keep, no matter how good our intentions. The fact that we should not acquire commitments we are not competent to keep has important implications for what trustworthiness demands of us, given the connection between trust and commitment: the demands of trustworthiness are the topic of chapter 4.

Additional Sources

1.1 Trust and Reliance. Simon (2013) and McLeod (2015) provide very useful overviews and bibliographic guidance into philosophical literature about trust. Hawley (2012) is a whistle-stop tour of different disciplinary approaches to trust, and Hardin (2002) is a more advanced introduction. Hawley (2014a) is the basis for much of the current chapter; it includes more detailed discussions of rival pictures, and more extensive reference to sources.

1.2 Distrust and Non-Reliance. Distrust is given philosophical centre stage less frequently than is trust; an important exception is the issue of distrust in politics. See Hardin (ed.) (2004), Krishnamurthy (2015), and other papers in the October 2015 issue of *The Monist* on Trust and Democracy. Some forms of epistemic injustice can be understood in terms of unfair distrust and its consequences; I return to these issues in chapter 6.

1.3 Reliance and Non-Reliance. Thompson (2017) resists the standard connections between trust and reliance. Govier (1993) understands trust in terms of vulnerability, as does Jones e.g. in her (2004).

1.4 The Commitment Account. For accounts of various different types of commitment, see Chang (2013), Calhoun (2009), and Holton (2009). Hollis (1998: 11) and Nickel (2007) link trust to obligation. For McLeod (2002) trust involves the expectation that the trustee will act out of moral integrity; McLeod's book is an important discussion of self-trust. On the second-personal nature of trust, see especially Darwall (2017), and the sources listed below under section 1.8.

1.5 Looking Beyond Expectations. Strawson (1974) introduces the notion of the 'participant stance' as invoked by Holton. In later work Jones develops her views of trust in many interesting ways, e.g. (2004), (2012), (2013). On the importance of getting it right about trust and distrust, see e.g. Fricker (2007), Jones (2002), and Marsh (2011); I return to this issue in chapters 5 and 6.

1.6 Why Commitment Rather than Motives. Other accounts in terms of motive are reviewed by McLeod (2015).

1.7 Betrayal. Jones (2004) usefully writes of 'basal (in)security' in this context, whilst Sunstein (2007) discusses our aversion to 'betrayal risk', though without strictly marking the trust-reliance distinction. Ratcliffe, Ruddell, and Smith (2014) explore connections between trauma and trust.

1.8 Where Next? For resistance to taking three-place trust as basic, see Domenicucci and Holton (2017), Faulkner (2015), and Faulkner (2017).

2

Promising

Commitment is at the heart of my preferred notions of trust and distrust. But where do our commitments come from? In chapter 5, I will explore a range of less explicit ways in which our speech and action generate commitments relevant to the realm of trust and distrust. But in the present chapter I focus on promise-making, the most explicit mechanism through which we take on new commitments. Trusting someone to keep a promise is a high-stakes, central case of trust, whilst anticipating that someone will break a promise is a paradigmatic case of distrust.

In thinking about promises and trust, obvious questions include how to decide who to trust, whose promises to accept and rely upon. And in thinking about these questions, we typically take on the perspective of the promise-receiver. But my central concern in this chapter arises primarily from the perspective of the promise-giver, rather than the promise-receiver. If we aspire to be trustworthy, we aspire to be good promisors; bad promisors are untrustworthy people. So what do good promisors do? They keep their promises. But not only this: they make the right promises in the first place.

Promises are offered and accepted in the spirit of hope, whilst a broken promise is a sad business. And not just sad, but bad: breaking a promise is not the worst crime imaginable, yet it is paradigmatically wrong, unless there are extenuating circumstances. We may regret our promises, but regret alone cannot release us from the moral obligation to follow through on our words. This much is evident, even though it is less evident exactly why promises have the moral force they do, and very far from evident what qualifies circumstances as extenuating.

It is also evident, though less commonly remarked, that a promise can be bad without being a broken promise: some promises should not have been made in the first place, even if they are eventually kept. For example, it is prima facie wrong to make an insincere promise, even if a

How To Be Trustworthy. Katherine Hawley, Oxford University Press (2019). © Katherine Hawley.
DOI: 10.1093/oso/9780198843900.001.0001

later change of heart or change of circumstance reconciles the promisor to acting as she promised. Moreover a promise to act immorally is itself prima facie immoral, and not because it is a broken promise. Indeed, given that such a promise has been made, breaking it may be the least bad option.

Insincerity and immoral intent: who could deny that these are nasty traits? But bad promises can sometimes be rooted in the very best of intentions, in an optimistic desire to be helpful. A reckless or incompetent promise—a promise to perform the infeasible—is a promise which should not have been made, even if it is, by some miracle, eventually kept rather than broken. Or so I will argue in this chapter.

How will I try to persuade you? By describing cases in which a promise should not have been made, even though it is a sincere promise to do something permissible, and it is eventually kept rather than broken. But various issues muddy the water. First, we may disagree about what it takes for a promise to be sincere, and about what it takes for a promised action to be permissible. Second, we should recognize that maintaining a hygienic practice of promise-making is not always of paramount importance. Making an insincere or reckless promise might sometimes be the best option, all things considered; indeed, being untrustworthy might sometimes be the best option, all things considered. Third, we should distinguish between our assessment of a promise and our assessment of the promise-maker. For example, someone might reasonably but falsely believe that her promise is permissible, in which case we may love the sinner whilst hating the sin. These last two issues are not distinctively associated with promise-making: analogous concerns arise whenever we discuss norms and evaluations for our practices. Important goals can come into conflict with one another, and we can in general distinguish between whether someone has violated a norm and whether she could reasonably have been expected to know that she has violated a norm.

Moreover we may reasonably disagree about the type of normativity in question here. It seems clear that the obligation to keep one's promises is a moral obligation. Indeed, it is a central, paradigmatic case of moral obligation. But what about the norms which govern promise-*making*? In chapter 3 I will argue for a close connection between norms on assertion—purporting to provide information to others—and norms on promise-making. Since norms on assertion are not standardly thought of as moral norms, this might suggest that norms on promise-making are not moral norms. I will suggest, however, that we should make the opposite inference, understanding the moral dimensions of assertion in terms of its connection to promising.

For lots of reasons, then, we may disagree about the exact content of norms on promise-making, and about the source or nature of those norms. But that's okay. My main goal in this chapter is to illuminate the importance of competence in good promise-making, and conversely to explain what is wrong with reckless or incompetent promise-making. I will argue that, no matter how we articulate the sincerity norm, and the norm that one should not promise to do something which is itself immoral, these do not exhaust the norms on promise-making. Instead, there is a third way in which promise-making can go wrong: roughly speaking, one should not make promises which one is not competent to keep. The paired notions of recklessness and competence need closer scrutiny, but my first task is to show that something like this third norm is needed, because there are sincere promises to act permissibly which nevertheless should not be made.

2.1 Sincerity

Insincere—'false'—promises are bad promises. If Ruth insincerely promises to come to Kenton's party, privately intending to stay at home in front of the TV, she thereby violates a norm of promise-making: that's not the kind of promise you should make. Suppose Ruth later changes her mind, either because of a pang of conscience or because there's nothing much on TV. She shows up for the party, thus keeping her promise. Well, better than not showing up, we may say. Still, Ruth is at fault for having made an insincere promise, and Kenton in particular may be cross if he discovers what Ruth did. Showing up—keeping the promise—doesn't automatically wipe the slate clean.

Now, extenuating circumstances may make insincere promising permissible or even required, all things considered: insincerely promising to come to a party seems okay if it is a cover for your secret hostage rescue mission. Nevertheless, making an insincere promise should be the source of some regret: all else being equal, it would be better if you could rescue the hostages without needing to make an insincere promise. Insincere promises fall short as promises, even when they are permitted or even mandated on other grounds.

What is it for a promise to be insincere? A natural thought is that a sincere promise communicates the promise-maker's genuine intentions, and so a promise is insincere when the promise-maker lacks the intention communicated by the promise. But philosophers disagree about what intention is communicated by a promise. For example Scanlon (1998: 307) argues that a promise to do something communicates an intention to do that very thing: when Ruth promises to come to the party, she communicates her purported intention to come to the party. (That's not all she does, but it's an important part of what's going on.) Then an insincere promise is one made without the corresponding intention to act.

In contrast, Owens (2012: chapter 8) argues that a promise essentially communicates not an intention to act, but the intention to place oneself under an obligation to act. Suppose Tony promises Pat that he will help with the harvest, although he does not intend to help with the harvest because he assumes that Pat will later release him from his promise. So long as Tony intends to become obliged to help with the harvest, then Owens will classify his promise as sincere. Marušić (2015) argues for a third account of sincerity: for him, a sincere promise must be underpinned not merely by an appropriate intention, but by a belief that the promise will be kept. As Marušić shows, this raises all sorts of intriguing issues about how such a belief may be rational in situations where evidence suggests we're likely to be tempted to break our promise.

There are many subtleties here, for example around the differences between having an intention and foreseeing that you will acquire an intention. Sometimes, it seems, we make a promise in an effort to acquire an intention we wish we had. Fortunately, these subtleties are not important for my purposes here, and neither is the issue of exactly which intention is communicated by a promise. This is because sincerity is not my main focus in the context of this book. I will argue that a promise can be a bad promise even when the promisor has all the good intentions and attitudes which might be thought relevant, including an intention to act, an intention to become obliged to act, and a belief that the promise will be kept.

Might we unwittingly make insincere promises, falsely but reasonably believing ourselves to be sincere? If so, then we should distinguish subjective from objective dimensions of evaluation. When Jill reasonably believes that she intends to go to the gym, although she does not in fact intend to go to the gym, she may be blameless in promising to do so. Likewise if she falsely but reasonably believes she believes she will go to the gym. Nevertheless there is an important sense in which Jill should not have made the promise. With the benefit of hindsight, Jill might reasonably say 'I realize now that I didn't really mean to go to the gym, so I shouldn't have promised to do so'. In chapters 4 and 5, I will discuss what kind of self-knowledge we need in order to be trustworthy.

Insincere promises are sometimes kept, just as sincere promises are sometimes broken. If an insincere promise-maker eventually keeps her promise, we may regard the person as having redeemed matters somewhat. Nevertheless, we may still criticize the initial promise, and indeed the person concerned should look back with some regret. We care about whether promises are sincere, as well as whether they are eventually kept or broken.

2.2 Promising to Behave Badly

What else do we care about? Sometimes a promise is wrong because it is a promise to act immorally. Such promises are test cases for whether promising to do something inevitably generates at least some obligation to do it. On the one hand, the central point of promising is that it generates obligations; but on the other hand, surely an immoral act does not inch closer to becoming obligatory when we promise to do it. The broader context for this debate is the issue of how promises generate obligations to act. Can we—should we?—derive an 'ought' from the 'is' of promising?

But we can recognize that we should not promise to act immorally, regardless of whether such promises generate obligations. For starters, if the immoral action involves a harm to others then a public promise is in effect a threat, and can be condemned on those grounds. Even where others are not immediately threatened, we should not promise to act immorally. On the one hand, if making such promises generates even a weak, outweighable, obligation to do something immoral, this counts against making such promises. On the other hand, if such promises do not generate obligations, they would still be problematic. Suppose the person promising to act immorally intends to keep her promise: then she is criticizable on those grounds. Suppose that the person intends only to become obliged to act immorally (as Owens would require for sincerity): it seems perverse to try to put oneself in this position. Suppose instead she has no such intentions: then the promise is insincere. Whichever way we look at them, promises to act immorally are bad news.

As before, extenuating circumstances may make promising to act immorally permissible or even required, all things considered. To take a standard type of example, suppose an undercover police agent promises to assassinate a criminal's rival, hoping with this promise to gain the criminal's trust. Assassinating the rival would be immoral. But merely promising to do so does not seem so bad, might even be morally required if this were the only way to further the investigation. In such cases, it's hard to imagine the agent having any kind of regret about having made the promise. But this is because the criminal is not worthy of the usual respect due to others. If instead the agent ends up promising to an innocent bystander that she will perform some immoral act, this should inspire some regret even if overall it would be the right thing to do.

As with the sincerity norm, we can assess the promise but we can also assess what the promise-maker reasonably believed about her promise. Suppose Jolene promises to do something which she reasonably but mistakenly believes to be morally permissible. We might exonerate her from blame, but nevertheless maintain that in some objective sense this promise should not have been made. Indeed Jolene herself should regret the promise once she appreciates the immorality of the act, even if she recognizes that she is not blameworthy.

Holly M. Smith (1997) considers a principle somewhat like the norm I am proposing:

> Prohibition Principle: If an act would be wrong, all things considered (independent of any promise to perform it), then it would be wrong, all things considered, to promise to perform that act. (158)

Smith argues that the Prohibition Principle is falsified by cases such as the undercover agent, where the promise is not all-things-considered wrong, even though assassinating the rival would itself be wrong. More controversially, Smith also argues, aligning herself with Henry Sidgwick, that 'a promise can be morally permissible even in cases where the promised act occurs and would be wrong were it not for the promise' (159). That is, promising and then keeping a promise may be the overall best option, even though it would have been wrong to take the action in question had it not been promised. For example, it might be best overall for a politician to make (and keep) a promise to implement a wasteful policy, if that's what it takes for her to win the election and implement a host of good policies.

In effect, Smith advocates a norm on promise-making which is weaker than the Prohibition Principle: she endorses promises like the politician's wasteful pledge, which the simple norm condemns. Fortunately, I do not need to resolve this issue. My aim is to show that there are promises which should not be made even though they satisfy very high standards of sincerity and morality-of-promised-action, because we also assess promises on a third dimension—that of competence.

2.3 Competence

A good promise requires both a sincere intention and the permissibility of the action promised. But these together are not enough—sometimes we go wrong by promising too much, even though we sincerely intend to live up to our words and believe that we will. After all, it is easy to misjudge either our own capacities or else what it will take to keep a given promise. But what counts as over-promising? How cautious do we need to be?

Julia Driver (1983, 2011) discusses cases where people promise too much, intentionally or unintentionally. Sometimes a person makes conflicting promises and cannot keep them all, although any individual promise could be kept at the expense of the others. Sometimes a person makes an individual promise which simply cannot be kept. Driver's main concern is whether unkeepable promises generate obligations. If they do, this undermines the idea that 'ought' implies 'can': the promisor ends up with an obligation to do something she can't in fact do. If they don't, this undermines the claim that promises inevitably generate some type or degree of obligation. For my purposes, however, it matters only that such unkeepable promises should not have been made in the first place; moreover, I will not distinguish individual and collective unkeepability, important though the distinction may be elsewhere.

Call this the 'keepability norm': do not make promises that you cannot keep (don't write cheques you can't cash). As with other norms, we should concede that the keepability norm can be overridden by other considerations, most obviously in extreme circumstances where good promising is not the foremost goal. If making an unkeepable promise is the only way to save the world, then you should go right ahead and promise. Moreover we can again distinguish subjective from objective evaluation, separating the question whether a promise-maker reasonably believes her promise to be keepable from the question whether the promise is indeed keepable.

What's wrong with unkeepable promises? It seems almost too obvious to say, but if you make a promise which is unkeepable you condemn yourself to breaking a promise, thus violating the basic requirement not to break promises. This marks a difference from the other norms I discussed above: an insincere promise may nevertheless be kept, as may a promise to act immorally. There are no unkeepable promises which are nevertheless kept.

But we sometimes over-promise even though the promises we make are individually and even collectively keepable: mere keepability is too weak a constraint. Imagine that a child is brought into hospital, very sick, with an unidentified, unfamiliar condition. The junior doctor overseeing the case promises the parents that she will save their child's life, and this is what she sincerely intends to do. It turns out that the child's condition can be treated with a particular type of antibiotic, which the doctor happens to try first, and so the doctor saves the child's life. Great! Still, a more experienced physician may rightly criticize the junior doctor for having made such a rash promise: after all, she had no idea what condition the child was suffering from, nor whether it would turn out to be treatable. The doctor could have promised to try her best to save the child. But she should not have simply and recklessly promised to save the child.

Likewise, we can imagine reckless promises to track down a mysterious criminal, or to win an Olympic medal some day, or to learn to speak Polish with no trace of an accent; in each case we can imagine that the promise is kept, against the odds. These are promises to do permissible, indeed admirable, deeds. Such promises could be made sincerely: it's easy to imagine someone genuinely—optimistically—intending to do these things, not just intending to try. Indeed, it's fairly easy to imagine someone genuinely, optimistically believing that she will successfully do these things, as Marušić (2015) requires for sincerity. The promises are keepable, indeed the promises are kept. Nevertheless, they seem problematic—this is over-promising.

In all these cases, the promise is a sincere commitment to do something which is both practically possible and morally permissible. Moreover, the promise-maker can reasonably believe that all this is so. The junior doctor knows that she intends to save the child, and that this would be a wonderful outcome. And she can quite reasonably believe that it is possible to save the child's life. After all, the child is still alive on arrival at the hospital, which is full of medical personnel, drugs and equipment. So the doctor satisfies the keepability norm, and moreover she reasonably believes that she satisfies the norm, and thus is not criticizable on this count.

The trouble is that mere keepability—the mere possibility of keeping the promise—doesn't seem enough, and likewise reasonable belief in mere keepability doesn't suffice to vindicate the promise-maker. We evaluate promise-making by a more demanding standard. But what is this more demanding standard? An attractive first thought is that, since the mere possibility of keeping the promise is not enough, perhaps what's required is that the promise will in fact be kept: other things being equal, a good promise is one which will be kept, and a bad promise is one which will be broken.

A first challenge to this first thought is that the junior doctor *does* keep her promise, *does* successfully save the child's life. Likewise, we imagined the detective, the Olympic hopeful, and the aspiring Polish speaker as successfully keeping their promises, against the odds. What, then, has gone wrong in such cases? This first challenge is met by distinguishing our evaluation of the promise from our evaluation of the promise-maker. Although such promises are good, because they will be kept, the promise-makers themselves are reckless, because they cannot reasonably believe that their promises will be kept, cannot reasonably believe that they satisfy the will-be-kept norm. The junior doctor saves the child, and reasonably believed that this was possible. But if she believed that she would in fact save the child, that belief was not justified.

A tougher challenge is this. We can imagine various sorts of cases in which someone makes a sincere promise to do something permissible, that promise will be kept, and moreover the promisor reasonably believes that all this is so; yet the promise is a bad promise. These cases are structurally analogous to cases in which someone has a true, justified belief and yet lacks knowledge.

Here is one sort of case. Suppose that Usha promises to buy Alan a pint of the best beer in Borsetshire, but has no idea which this is. She takes advice from the confident-seeming barman, and so she reasonably believes she will buy the best beer. But the barman is brand new, knows nothing about beer, and picks the best one merely by luck. So Usha keeps her promise: she buys Alan a pint of the best beer in Borsetshire. And Usha is quite reasonable in her belief that she is keeping her promise: it's perfectly reasonable for her to take advice about beer from the barman, who does seem to know what he is talking about.

Still, the promise seems problematic. You may be sceptical about my evasive use of 'problematic'. As a stopgap, consider how Usha might feel later when she grasps the true situation. She might think that she had a lucky escape, that if she had known the barman was a novice she would not have made the promise, and that that would have been safer; she might regret making the promise, even knowing that she did manage to keep it. This is not an ideal promise: we shouldn't make a habit of promising in this style, and should take steps to avoid such promising.

Here is a different sort of case. Faced with taking a ball at random from an urn containing 999 red balls and one black, Sid reasonably believes that he will pull out a red ball, and so he does. But he should not promise to do so; if he did promise, we'd suspect he had rigged the draw. If Sid promised to draw a red ball, he would be sincerely promising to do something permissible, he would keep his promise, and he would reasonably believe all this is so. Still, this is not the sort of promise he ought to make, not an ideal promise.

When they make their promises, Usha and Sid each have a reasonable true belief in their own success. But their beliefs do not amount to knowledge. So it is tempting to suppose that good promising requires not just success, and reasonable belief about success, but full-blown knowledge that one will successfully keep the promise. There is a really bad way and an only slightly better way to spell out this suggestion. The really bad way is to build a knowledge requirement into our 'subjective' evaluation of the promise-maker, to argue that a good promise is one which will be kept, and a good promise-maker is someone who knows her promise is good. This is a bad move because half the point of separating subjective and objective evaluations is to exonerate people who blamelessly violate an underlying norm. If blamelessness requires knowledge that the norm is satisfied, then blameless violations of the norm will be impossible.

The only slightly better way is to strengthen the norm itself: do not make promises unless you know you will keep them. (The corresponding 'subjective' evaluation would assess whether the promise-maker reasonably believed she knew she would keep her promise.) Although this is slightly better, it is nevertheless not much good, because it imposes an enormously stringent requirement on promise-making. Indeed, on reflection we might think that even the original success requirement is too strong, that there are perfectly good promises which nevertheless are eventually broken. This is not to say that it is sometimes good to break a promise, though that may also be true if the circumstances are extreme. The thought is that a promise's being broken does not inevitably mean that it should not have been made in the first place; one might regret breaking a promise yet not regret having made the promise, even with hindsight.

This is a tricky business, as is reflected by some complicated remarks from J. L. Austin:

> you are prohibited from saying 'I promise I will, but I may fail'...
> [however] 'but I may fail' does not mean merely 'but I am a weak human being' (in which case it would be no more exciting than adding 'D.V.' ['God willing']): it means that there is some concrete reason for me to suppose that I shall break my word. It is naturally always possible ('humanly' possible) that I...may break my word, but that by itself is not bar against using the expression... 'I promise'.   (1946: 170)

Austin makes these remarks whilst discussing the impropriety of saying 'I know it is so, but I may be wrong'; such claims are not my direct focus here. But I take two main points from what Austin says. First, there is something like a performative contradiction in saying out loud 'I promise I will, but there is some concrete reason for me to suppose that I shall break my word'. Of course, it may be true that you promise even though there is concrete reason for you to think that you will break your promise, so there is no outright inconsistency here. But there is something self-undermining about putting things this way. In my view, this reflects the existence of a competence norm on promise-making: to acknowledge that there is a concrete reason to think you will not succeed is to acknowledge your lack of proper competence in this regard. Thus you simultaneously announce your promise and announce that you are violating a norm of promising.

Marušić (2015) offers an alternative explanation of why it is problematic to say 'I promise I will, but there is some concrete reason for me to suppose that I shall break my word'. In his view, this would reveal either that the promise is insincere, because the promisor does not believe that she will keep the promise, or else that the promise is based on an unreasonable belief that the promise will be kept, unreasonable because the promisor openly acknowledges that there is concrete reason not to believe this. Marušić's primary concern is the internal consistency of the promisor's stance regarding her commitments and future behaviour. As will emerge later, I am more concerned with the promisor's social situation, including the judgements of others regarding her competence, and I want to retain sight of the idea that a promise is a good one if based on underlying competence, even if the promisor herself is uncertain about this. She may be subjectively in a non-ideal state, but that does not automatically undermine the quality of her promise. Conversely, I want to retain sight of the issues around both Sid and Usha, who seem internally consistent and subjectively reasonable, yet make what seem from an external perspective to be problematic promises.

The second point I take from the Austin passage is that there is no performative contradiction in saying 'I promise I will, but I am a weak human being, at God's mercy'. This suggests that actually keeping a promise is not a condition of properly making it in the first place. Good promise-making is compatible with the outside chance of failure to keep the promise, through an act of God or through general human frailty. Again, this marks a contrast between my concerns and those of Marušić:

Balancing art

his central cases are those in which temptation, or insufficient trying, are the principal obstacles to success, rather than broader worldly (or other-worldly) challenges.

So mere keepability is not enough, and arguably actually keeping a promise is neither necessary (bad luck doesn't make a promise bad in retrospect) nor sufficient (good luck doesn't always make for a good promise). Instead, I suggest that something like competence to keep the promise is a norm on promise-making: do not make promises you are not competent to keep. I will now show how this accounts for the counterexamples to other proposed norms. And I will offer some clarification of what competence amounts to, but I will not offer anything approaching a reductive analysis of competence. (I return to related issues in section 5.2, where I discuss how best to individuate competences and how to match commitment to competence.)

Recall the case of the junior doctor, where obeying the keepability norm—and reasonably believing oneself to do so—is not enough. The doctor does not have insight into the child's condition, nor any unusual skill of diagnosing and treating such conditions (unlike, say, the protagonist of the TV drama *House*). It is through good fortune that she happened first to try the antibiotics which worked. The promise to save the child was keepable, and indeed kept, but the doctor was not competent to keep the promise. This is not to say that she was an incompetent doctor; the point is just that she, like most doctors other than House, lacks competence in this particular respect.

What about Usha and Sid? Usha kept her promise to buy the best beer in Borsetshire, relying upon the testimony of the novice barman, so succeeding only through good luck. My suggestion is that Usha did not succeed through exercise of her competence. Again, it's not that she is a totally incompetent beer buyer, who thinks that beer is sold by the gram at the library. Rather, she is was not competent to keep the specific promise she made. Sid reliably draws a red ball from the urn, but should not promise to do so. Why not? Because it is not competence at drawing red balls on demand that explains his success. Conversely, a competence norm can explain why promises which are broken through bad luck are not automatically bad promises. This is because competence is not an absolute guarantee of success: circumstances may be unusual in various

Sometimes but a four part on competence

ways which frustrate us in the exercise of our competence. So it is possible to satisfy the competence norm, thus making a good promise, even when the promise is not kept.

My suggestion is that promises are subject to a competence norm: do not make promises unless you are competent to keep them. As with the other norms, we should allow that incompetent promises may be all-things-considered permissible if the stakes are high, and we should also distinguish the question of competence from the question of whether the promise-maker reasonably believed that she was competent to keep the promise.

What, then, is competence? Just as I failed to offer a reductive account of commitment, I will fail to offer a reductive account of competence. But this is unsurprising, given that most of us have given up trying to offer reductive accounts of notions such as knowledge. We can, however, identify a number of relevant features. Competence is a matter both of the person's intrinsic qualities and dispositions and also of the environment she finds herself in. Competence is not a guarantee of success, even when combined with good intentions: this explains why the success norm seems too strong in some circumstances. And lack of suitable competence may not amount to 'incompetence' in the normal sense: the junior doctor is a competent doctor, just as competent as her peers, but is nevertheless not competent to save a child with the unusual condition.

Is competence a statistical notion: do not promise unless there is a high probability you will succeed? Consideration of lottery situations suggests otherwise. Sid should not promise to draw a red ball, even though there is a high probability he will keep such a promise. On the other hand, a skilled baker's promise to make a delicious cake seems perfectly acceptable, even though there's some real chance that the oven will break down, or the power will fail.

Ernest Sosa has made sophisticated, fruitful use of the notion of competence in his epistemology. For Sosa, 'Competences are dispositions of an agent to perform well' (2010: 465), and, like dispositions generally, they have a three-part structure: constitution, condition, and situation. In the case of archery competence, these take in respectively 'the seat of the archer's skill', her being awake and sober, and the external circumstances, such as lighting and weather, which are conducive to success. Likewise, the competence required for good promise-making should encompass all three of these elements, including appropriate external circumstances, and not just internal constitution; the role of external circumstances will be a major theme in later chapters.

I will continue to treat competence as a kind of placeholder notion— we will be able to say a bit more about what kind of feature it is in the light of later discussions. My primary purpose is not to pin down an exact notion, but rather to get a good enough grip to be able to explore the connections to trustworthiness and to our social dealings around competence, knowledge, and judgements thereof. For now, the key points are that competence is not mere success, and nor is it mere justified belief about success: it is something like a steady, reliable capacity to achieve success. In the second half of this book I will be concerned with practical issues around competence, commitment, and trustworthiness: for the most part, answers to the interesting questions do not turn on precise formulations of the core terms.

My overarching goal in this chapter is to argue for the existence of this kind of third norm on promise-making. In the next chapter I will argue that there is a parallel norm on telling, or assertion-making. I will explain this parallel by arguing that assertion-making involves promise-making. This means that readers who prefer success to competence, or have specific views about competence, can stay on board to see what consequences their preference should have when it comes to assertion. It is philosophically contentious which norms govern assertion, so it should not be a surprise if the exact form and strength of the norms governing promise-making are equally open to dispute. Indeed these parallel disputes reinforce my claim that promise-making and assertion-making are linked.

That said, I do think that the competence norm is more plausible than the success norm. Part of my argument relied upon contestable intuitions about cases, such as Usha, Sid, the junior doctor, the skilled baker, and so on. Intuitions about such matters are especially prone to haziness, given the availability of both 'objective' and 'subjective' dimensions of evaluation: if a case seems intuitively problematic, is this because a norm has been violated, or because the promise-maker has not been careful enough about whether she satisfies the norm?

One way to circumvent this reliance on intuitions is to consider what norms for promise-making we should expect there to be, given the nature and source of our obligation to keep our promises. There are, of course, differing philosophical accounts of why we should keep our promises, and to some extent these correspond to variation in the detail of what we should say about the exact competence norm. I will not explore this issue in detail. But I will sketch how different accounts of promissory obligations might explain certain competence-related norms on promise-making. The literature on promising is strikingly concerned with the temptation to make insincere promises, whilst issues of incompetence or recklessness rarely reach the surface. Nevertheless, the concerns which direct us towards sincerity also direct us towards competence.

2.4 Why These Norms?

Promises typically generate obligations, and it would be very surprising if norms on promise-making were independent of this fact. Indeed, we might expect the nature and importance of norms on promise-making to derive from the nature and importance of the promise-keeping norm. So why is it that we should keep our promises?

T. M. Scanlon (1998: 300) identifies what he calls 'the principle of Due Care'.

> Principle D: One must exercise due care not to lead others to form reasonable but false expectations about what one will do when one has good reason to believe that they would suffer significant loss as a result of relying on these expectations.

Promising to do something can often give rise to reasonable expectations that one will act as promised, and often a promisee puts herself at risk of significant loss by relying upon a promisor. In such circumstances, principle D directs us to exercise due care not to make promises we will break. Scanlon focuses primarily on good intentions, but due care must also demand something like competence to act as promised.

As Scanlon shows however, Principle D seems to permit changes of mind about what we will do, so long as we warn others before they put themselves at risk of significant loss, or else compensate them for any loss incurred. But promises don't work that way: I cannot 'keep' my promise to do something either by warning you I will not do it after all or by compensating you for my failure to act. More generally, I am not released from my promise if it turns out you will suffer no significant loss if I do not keep my promise. Once I have promised to do something, my only option is to go ahead and do it, unless you release me.

Scanlon accounts for this in terms of the value of assurance, claiming that when expectations are raised, and assurance openly offered and accepted—as in a promise—then the assurer is obliged to act as expected. (Scanlon's Principle F (Scanlon 1998: 304) is more complex than this, but these elements are key for my purposes.) This in turn is justified by reference to Scanlon's contractualist moral theory, and the interest that we all have in being able to obtain, and to offer, assurance. Again, this points towards requirements both for an intention to perform and for competence to do so: 'assurance' is not the genuine assurance we value unless it is backed by competence, and the degree of competence required is all the greater where neither warning nor compensating are permissible options.

Rawls (1971) explains our obligation to keep promises in terms of fairness: since we have benefited in the past from the practice of promising, we would be free-riders if we now broke our promises. On this picture, the existence of sincerity and competence norms on promise-making is to be expected: if it were common practice to make incompetent promises, the institution of promising would not have the hoped-for benefits of helping 'to set up and to stabilize small-scale schemes of cooperation' (346), and without these benefits there would be no fairness-based reasons for us to keep our promises.

David Owens (2012) rejects both Scanlon's account and that of Rawls, arguing that the key function of promising is to transfer authority: when I promise you to do something, I give you authority over me in that respect. 'I maintain that promising exists because it serves our authority interest, our interest in having the right to oblige others to do certain things.' (146) Why should I ensure that I give you authority over me only in respect of things I am willing and able to do? A very general explanation is available here: perhaps I ought to make it the case that if I ought to do something then I do it. This explanation is general both in that it would apply to other situations in which we have some control over our obligations—not just through promise-making—and also in that it is available to Scanlon, Rawls, and others.

Does the notion of an authority interest suggest any more specific explanation of why promising might be governed by particular norms? Perhaps I can transfer authority only if I already have it myself, and perhaps there is a sense in which I myself do not have authority over whether I do something unless I am competent in that respect. Perhaps, but perhaps not: this line of thought (which I do not attribute to Owens) blurs normative authority together with practical control, and moreover suggests that it is simply impossible to make an incompetent promise.

Owens's account of promising in terms of our authority interest does not readily explain why promise-making should be governed by either a sincerity or a competence norm, except insofar as such norms may govern any voluntary acquisition of an obligation. This can be seen as a challenge either to Owens or to me. But Owens does acknowledge that in practice promising often does serve our information interest (our interest in giving and obtaining assurance), and he explains this in terms of the primary importance of the authority interest. Thus Owens can allow that promise-making will often be governed by the norms I have identified, even whilst denying that these are constitutive or essential to promise-making.

Scanlon, Rawls, and Owens do not exhaust the possibilities in this area, but they do represent important strands of thought about the nature of promising. With this express tour, I have merely sought to illustrate how these rival frameworks can give us different reasons to expect promise-making to be governed by certain kinds of norm, including both sincerity and competence.

We might now wonder what the source of this normativity is. Are these moral norms, whatever that means? Are we under a moral obligation to make sincere, competent promises if we make promises at all? Promises to act immorally are often referred to as 'immoral promises', or 'wicked promises', following J. E. J. Altham:

> The example I shall consider is of a promise to do something that there is a stringent obligation not to do. I call such promises wicked, thinking mainly of the wicked things that would be done if they were carried out, but recognising also the wickedness of making them, where the promisor is in a position to know what he is about. (1985: 1)

Is it likewise 'wicked' or at least morally wrong to make insincere or incompetent promises? I am inclined to think that it is. But one potential obstacle is that I want to understand norms on telling as a special cases of norms on promise-making, and it may seem contentious to regard norms on telling as moral norms. For that reason, I will return to this issue at the end of chapter 3, following my discussion of telling.

2.5 Offering to Promise

Throughout this chapter, I have discussed norms which govern promise-making, taking it for granted that these norms apply to the person making the promise, not to anyone else. But it takes two to promise. Making a promise generates an obligation to a particular person (or people) to whom the promise is made. And these obligations are not generated unless the promise is accepted. Often when someone says 'I promise to...' this is best understood as an irrevocable offer to take on promissory obligations, should the audience accept the offer. In some contexts, for example where a promise has been requested, acceptance is already in place. We see a similar pattern with offers to bet, offers to buy, and so on; this is no coincidence.

Is there any onus upon an audience to accept an offer only where the resulting promise satisfies the norms I have already discussed? Should you decline someone's offer to promise if you know that she is insincere, or incapable of keeping such a promise? In practice, all sorts of considerations will be in play, depending upon your relationship to the promise-offerer, whether she is a child or adult, the costs and benefits of causing her embarrassment either now or later, the interests of any third parties, and so on. Sometimes we can benefit when others wrong us (for example, when they break their promises to us); the moral high ground has many advantages. In general, it seems unduly demanding to suppose that we have obligations to prevent others from making bad promises to us.

Conversely, what about situations in which someone offers to promise, but the offer is not accepted, so no promise is made: are such situations governed by the norms of sincerity, competence, and permissibility-of-promised-action? Suppose first that the person making the offer knows that the offer will not be accepted. Even so, it seems to me, there is something problematic about holding oneself to lower standards in such a situation. The point about an offer is to put oneself at the disposal of the person to whom the offer is made, and one should not offer to do something one is not in a position to do, even if one knows the offer will be rejected. For example, I should not offer to give you something which does not belong to me, even if I know you will not accept my offer.

Suppose instead that the person making the offer is not in a position to know that the offer will be rejected. Then it seems even more clear that she should not offer a promise which would, if accepted, violate the norms of promise-making: she does not know that she will avoid violating those norms, and even if she did, as above, this does not seem to justify her behaviour.

I am not surveying all the possibilities here: we would need to distinguish different epistemic and doxastic situations for both parties, distinguish more rigorously between assessing the offerer's actions and assessing her blameworthiness, and perhaps be more careful about what exactly is required by sincerity. Nevertheless, I will continue to suppose that we should not even offer incompetent promises. The issue of offering promises which we do not expect to be accepted may seem rather niche. But it is relevant to a range of situations in which we offer (purported) information to others, through attempted testimony, assertion, or telling: this is the topic of the next chapter.

For now, I hope to have established the following points. Promise-making is governed by norms which derive from the norm that one should keep one's promises. These include a norm of competence: don't make promises you are not competent to keep, where competence requires both more and less than successful promise-keeping. Rival theories of why we ought to keep our promises provide foundations for different accounts of why it is we should not make promises we are not competent to keep. Since promise-making is a paradigmatic, though not entirely typical, situation in which we incur new commitments, these constraints on promise-making give us some insight into the demands of trustworthiness—I will explore this connection in chapter 4.

Admittedly, I have not pinned down exactly what it is to be competent in some respect, nor what it is to succeed through the exercise of competence. Yet it's clear that something of this sort is missing in cases where promises are problematic even though they are sincere. Appreciating the importance of competence for promise-making raises questions that I will explore in the remainder of the book. For example, how do we judge our own competence so as to become good promise-makers (which might sometimes mean declining to promise)? How do we judge others in respect of their promise-making skills, and how does this relate to judging their trustworthiness? Emphasis on the role of competence in good promise-making will also allow me to draw fruitful connections between promising and telling, the topic of chapter 3.

Additional Sources

2.1 Sincerity. Stokke (2014) discusses insincerity and conscious mental attitudes. D'Cruz and Kalef (2015) respond to Marušić's earlier articulation of his account in his (2013).

Shiffrin (2014) is an important contribution to these debates.

2.2 Promising to Behave Badly. Altham (1985) is an important discussion of 'wicked promises', whilst Searle (1969) focuses on the relationship between 'ought' and 'is' here.

2.3 Competence. The arguments for a competence norm on promising shadow Williamson's (2000: chapter 11) arguments for a knowledge norm on assertion, including lottery concerns, conversational patterns around assertion, and Moore's paradoxical claims. Usha's promise about beer-buying is analogous to the 'Gettiered' justified true belief of someone who falls short of knowledge (Gettier 1963). Hawley (2018b) takes up some analogous issues around competence and creativity. Hawthorne and Stanley (2008: 578) discuss the shakiness of intuitions about norm violations.

2.4 Why These Norms? There is an extensive philosophical literature about the nature of promising. Heuer (2012a, 2012b) provides a helpful review, and the essays in Sheinman (ed.) (2011) cover a lot of interesting ground.

2.5 Offering to Promise. Here I draw on (Owens 2006: 73) and (Thomson 1990: 298).

3

Telling

Trusting someone to keep her promises typically means trusting her as an agent, relying upon her to behave as she has committed to behaving. But not all trust concerns action: we also face important decisions about whose words to trust, in both private and public spheres. It is no coincidence that we speak of trust, distrust, and betrayal both in regard to speech and in regard to practical action. So, given my emphasis on commitment in connection with trust and distrust, it's important for me to show how trusting other people's words involves relying upon them to fulfil a commitment. The present chapter therefore focuses on trust and telling—that is, speech (or writing, or signing) which purports to offer reliable information to others.

In chapter 2, I argued that promise-making is governed by norms of sincerity, competence, and permissibility of what's promised. In this chapter, I will argue that we can understand telling as involving a promise to speak truthfully. And I will argue that telling is governed by norms of sincerity, competence, and permissibility of speaking truthfully on that matter. Across the two chapters, the cluster of claims is mutually supportive: it is independently plausible that telling is governed by such norms, and moreover this is just what we should expect if telling involves promising.

I am not the first to suggest that telling and promising are somehow connected. But, in my view, this connection has not previously been articulated in the most plausible fashion, and so has been vulnerable to easy objections. Exploring the connection also has a broader purpose in the context of this book. It helps us understand the way in which 'epistemic' or 'intellectual' trust, distrust, and trustworthiness are related to their practical counterparts: trusting someone to speak truthfully is a special case of trusting him or her to do something. This will allow me to move between epistemic and practical concerns in later chapters

How To Be Trustworthy. Katherine Hawley, Oxford University Press (2019). © Katherine Hawley.
DOI: 10.1093/oso/9780198843900.001.0001

more easily, and to explore what obstacles there are to trustworthiness in each domain.

3.1 Telling and Asserting

I am interested in situations where people purport to offer information in a relatively serious fashion (although the information itself may be trivial), presenting it as truthful. We make assertions, testify, and tell each other things, and there has been plenty of recent philosophical discussion of such activity, cast in quite varying terminology. Telling seems often to be regarded as something we do in, through, or by making an assertion to an audience, whereas it is possible to make an assertion with no audience around. On this picture, we assert without telling when writing in a private diary or soliloquizing on the windswept moors. But different philosophers writing on these topics use terms in different ways. Even if assertion is possible without an audience on some particular occasion, it is nevertheless a social practice generated by our need to give information to one another.

The social nature of language and communication means that in practice we do not exercise absolute authority over what we do with our words. We may sometimes make commitments we did not anticipate, or fail to make commitments we intended to incur. We can incur commitment through speech even when we do not present ourselves as making serious assertion—for example by failing to object to a suggestion, by asking loaded questions, or by our choice between apparent synonyms. But I will defer these complications and grey areas to chapter 5, and focus in this chapter on more straightforward assertion or telling.

There is a tangle of issues and terminology here, and my main concern is to extract the notion which is most useful for thinking about trust, distrust, trustworthiness, and competence. If we focused solely on trust, it might seem that the core situation is one in which someone offers (purported) information, or offers to do something, and in consequence others come to rely upon the speaker. Thus it might seem that the interesting issues arise only once the speech is somehow properly received by an audience. But, as elsewhere, we should also keep distrust in focus whilst theorizing. If the speaker knows that she will be distrusted, does she have any obligations to speak truthfully? What if the speaker knows that she will simply be ignored, not treated as eligible for either trust or distrust? Indeed, issues of trustworthiness arise even before anyone speaks, as we consider who to ask for their opinion, or who to ask for practical help.

These concerns connect naturally with the issues around promising and offering to promise which I discussed at the end of chapter 2. To explore them properly, I first need to explain how and why, in my view, asserting or telling involves a kind of promise, and so I will return to these issues later in this chapter. For now, I will stick to the terminology of 'assertion' rather than 'telling', mainly because this fits with the majority of the authors I engage with. But the paradigm case is one in which an assertion is made to an audience, and involves at least an attempt to tell someone something.

3.2 Connecting Asserting with Promising

Assertion is a way of speaking seriously, more so than in play-acting, sleep-talk, or speculation; many philosophers have thought that asserting involves taking responsibility for something, or making a commitment of some kind, or offering something to the audience. So it is not a coincidence that there are norms governing the assertions we may make. Moral issues around lying and the norm of sincerity have been debated since philosophy began; contemporary debate has dwelt on whether we ought to *know* what we are talking about, as well as sincerely *believing* what we say.

Likewise, promise-making is a serious business, which involves taking responsibility, or committing, or offering, and which is governed by norms, as I discussed in chapter 2. But if we try to assimilate asserting to promise-making, we seem to face an unattractive dilemma. Philosophical accounts of promising standardly focus on promising to do something, whereas asserting seems to be a matter of asserting that something is true. So if we want to treat assertion as a form of promise, then either we have to assimilate asserting *that* to promising *that*, or else we have to work out what we are promising *to do* when we make an assertion.

The first of these options is not attractive. Asserting that the front door is locked amounts to something less than promising that the front door is locked. Someone who promises that the door is locked needs to be in a stronger epistemic situation than does someone who asserts that the door is locked. She seems to be taking more responsibility onto her own shoulders when she promises, and this is why we sometimes ask people to promise that something is true, even when they have already asserted it—sometimes we want more than just an assertion.

But the second option—identifying assertion with a promise to do something—can seem problematic too. In particular, where a proposition concerns the speaker's future behaviour, the difference between promising to do something and asserting is crucial: if I promise to come to your party, then (barring emergencies) I am obliged to come to your party, whilst if I assert that I will come to your party, then at most I am obliged to inform you if my plans change. Promising to do something seems to be more charged with responsibility than merely asserting or predicting that I will do it.

So it is tempting to account for assertion in terms of promising, but difficult to see how. My preference is for the second option, that is, the claim that asserting involves promising to do something. I need to show how we can take this option whilst recognizing the difference between my promising to do something and merely asserting that I will do that very thing. That is the central task of this chapter.

I claim that asserting as to whether p involves both

(a) promising to speak truthfully as to whether p; and

(b) speaking truthfully or untruthfully as to whether p, i.e. keeping or breaking the promise.

I focus on 'asserting as to whether p'; this contrasts with the more standard focus on 'asserting that p' or 'asserting p'. But what is it to assert as to whether p? As I stipulatively use the phrase, there are two ways to do this: either one asserts that p, or one asserts that not-p. To make an assertion as to whether the front door is locked, I must either assert that the front door is locked, or assert that the front door is not locked.

There are various other assertions one might make about whether the front door is locked. One might assert that it's insignificant whether the front door is locked, unknown whether the front door is locked, even taboo to discuss whether the front door is locked. One might assert that it's probable that the front door is locked, or possible that the front door is locked. But for my purposes none of these will count as asserting as to whether the front door is locked.

'Speaking' here is a neutral term, which could be substituted by 'writing' or 'signing' (e.g. in BSL or ASL). Speaking as to whether p can be done without asserting—e.g. as part of a game, or whilst performing in a play. A speaker speaks truthfully as to whether p if she says that p and p is true, or if she says that not-p and not-p is true: speaking truthfully requires match between words and world, rather than words and beliefs. (Where beliefs are the topic of conversation, then beliefs are part of the world, in the relevant sense.)

This means that, on my view, assertion involves a promise to speak in ways which in fact match the world, not merely to do one's best on this front. Assertions are therefore faulty when they are in fact false, even if the speaker could not have known this, indeed even if nobody could have known the truth of this matter. In my view this is an advantage of the account, since factually inaccurate assertions are indeed faulty; more broadly this fits with the themes of chapters 4, 5, and 6, where I explore how we can unwittingly become untrustworthy. Nevertheless, unintentional falsehoods are usually treated with more sympathy than intentional lies; I return to questions of blame and criticism later in this chapter.

I claim that assertion involves a promise, but it is not only a promise: assertion also involves keeping or breaking that very promise. So the promise made in assertion is unusual, because it is simultaneously made and kept, or else simultaneously made and broken. More usually, a promise binds us to act at some later time, specified or unspecified, somehow offering assurance to others about our future behaviour. (We can accept that promises often assure without determining whether this is constitutive of their role.) One reason to value this assurance is that guidance and insight about the future are otherwise in short supply, especially where others' free actions are concerned.

But it is not only the future which can be hidden from us. Often the audience for an assertion lacks independent access to whether what is said is true. This explains why a promise to speak truthfully can be valuable in such a case. Even though it is simultaneously kept or broken, it is not is immediately obvious which of these has occurred, and so the fact that the speaker has promised to speak truthfully offers assurance of the truth of what's said.

Here is a different example of a promise which is simultaneously made and kept-or-broken. Clarrie asks Eddy 'Do you promise to say your next word as loudly as you can?' Eddy shouts back 'YES!' but it is not obvious whether this is his maximum volume. Eddy promises to speak as loudly as he can manage, and simultaneously either keeps or breaks the promise. For Clarrie the promise has the same value as it would if it were a promise about some future state of affairs.

Could a promise be kept by a past action? Suppose that Shula is anxious for Elizabeth to destroy a private diary for her. Elizabeth has already destroyed the diary, but explaining this would be complicated or embarrassing. Instead, she simply says 'Yes, I promise to destroy the diary'. There is something misleading about this, since it at least implicates that the deed has not yet been done (perhaps Elizabeth could weaken this by saying instead 'I promise to ensure that the diary is destroyed'). Moreover it's not the most informative thing which Elizabeth could say, given the circumstances. Nevertheless, it functions to assure Shula much as a promise would do, and it looks more like a kept promise than a broken promise. Can we identify what Elizabeth says with a promise that she has destroyed the diary? No, but I will wait until section 3.5 before discussing what it is to promise that something is the case.

I don't need to insist that such retrospective 'promises' are indeed promises. But I do put weight on the ideas that promises can be simultaneously made and kept-or-broken, and that such promises can be valuable to an audience. I hope that readers who still cannot accept that such simultaneously kept-or-broken commitments are genuine promises will nevertheless be able to understand my claims in this chapter as concerning the type of commitments which are typically generated by promises, which come with the norms and social role promises typically involve.

Does simultaneity collapse any distinction between a promise and a mere offer to promise? After all, in chapter 2 I endorsed the view that promissory obligations are generated only when promises are accepted. But, as I noted then, an offer to promise may be immediately binding if acceptance has been indicated ahead of time: if I ask you to promise, then I don't need to specify later that I accept your promise, since my acceptance is implicit in my request. Even where it's less clear whether the audience will accept what's offered, a promise-offerer needs to be cautious, acting on the assumption that the offer to promise will receive uptake, since it will be too late to change matters once this becomes clear. If a promise must be simultaneously kept, in order to be kept at all, then the promise-offerer must act to keep the promise; in this case, to speak truthfully.

To help make the case for this promise-based account of assertion, I will show how the proposal differs from the stronger view, associated with Brandom (1983), that assertion involves a commitment to defend-or-retract in the future. I will also show how the proposal can explain why testimony—offering information to others—involves 'assurance', but that it doesn't entail that such assurance has a distinctive epistemic significance. And I will show how this proposal differs from the discredited idea that an assertion that the front door is locked is simply a promise that the front door is locked.

3.3 Asserting and Committing

It is widely thought that asserting involves taking responsibility, making oneself accountable, making a commitment, or undertaking something. For Peirce, 'to assert a proposition is to make oneself responsible for its truth' (1932: 384). For Searle an assertion of p 'counts as an undertaking to the effect that p represents an actual state of affairs' (1969: 66). For Alston, an assertion that p involves a speaker's taking responsibility for its being the case that p (2000: 120); more generally, Alston understands a whole variety of speech in terms of the speaker's taking responsibility for the satisfaction of relevant conditions. For Williamson, 'To make an assertion is to confer a responsibility (on oneself) for the truth of its content; to satisfy the rule of assertion, by having the requisite knowledge, is to discharge that responsibility, by epistemically ensuring the truth of the content.' (2000: 268–9). For Williamson, the relevant responsibility is simultaneously self-conferred and discharged in the very act of assertion: likewise on my account everything happens at once, as a promise is simultaneously made and kept-or-broken.

According to 'commitment accounts' of assertion, in contrast, the responsibility extends beyond the moment of assertion. Brandom suggests 'taking the commitment involved in asserting to be the undertaking of justificatory responsibility for what is claimed' (1983: 641): to assert p is to become committed to justifying the claim that p, if challenged to do so. In his (2005) MacFarlane says that 'commitment to withdraw the assertion if and when it is shown to have been untrue' (318) is also involved: retraction in the face of counter-evidence fulfils a commitment made in assertion, rather than abandoning it. This is the same general notion of commitment as I used in chapter 1 in setting out my commitment account of trust and distrust. That is, it is not the psychological sense of having a determined intention—one can have a commitment in this sense whilst having no intention of fulfilling the commitment.

In contrast, more recently MacFarlane writes that the commitment view 'offers a simple and natural account of retraction, as the act of backing out of a commitment to the truth of the asserted proposition' (2011: 91). This makes sense only if we understand commitment as a kind of determined intention, rather than something which generates obligations to others: retraction is often legitimate, whereas promise-like commitments cannot legitimately and unilaterally be abandoned. More charitably, we can read MacFarlane as pointing out that once you retract an assertion, you are no longer obliged to justify it. Then on this view commitment to truth is best understood as commitment to either justify or retract.

My view that asserting involves promising to speak truthfully is a version of the idea that asserting involves taking responsibility for the truth of what is said. However it does not entail that assertion involves commitments which reach beyond the moment of making the assertion, with regard either to justification or retraction. Let me explain.

My account does not entail that assertion involves commitment to go on and justify. People who promise to do something become obliged to do it; they do not thereby become obliged to provide evidence of having done so if challenged. My son promises to finish his homework before dinner without thereby agreeing to show me the completed homework: he can keep his promise without showing me that he has done so. Likewise, a promise to speak truthfully is kept by speaking truthfully;

speakers are not required in addition to provide evidence that they have spoken truthfully, even if challenged.

So assertions do not automatically involve justificatory commitments, on my view. But we can appreciate why speakers are often under pressure to justify their assertions if challenged. My son fulfils his obligations—keeps his promise—even though he does not show me his homework. My main concern is that he do his homework, but I would also like assurance on this front, so that I can relax: I value my son's promise more if he is also willing to show me the completed homework. Likewise, assertions are often more valuable to the audience, and thus indirectly to the speaker, where they are accompanied by a justificatory commitment. So it is not surprising if assertions often come with this extra commitment, even though the commitment is not incurred merely by asserting.

Such situations involve many social complexities. Perhaps my son refuses to show his homework because he wants me to trust him, to take him at his word. Perhaps my inability to relax otherwise does reveal a lack of trust, but my son's refusal to offer assurance makes trusting even harder. More generally an assertion which does not come accompanied with a commitment to later justify does seem to embody a kind of challenge to the audience: take it or leave it, trust me or don't. When we hear a surprising assertion, we may ask in response 'how do you know?' But it's not obvious that we are entitled to an answer to that question.

What about retraction? Suppose I promise to lock the door when leaving your house, but forget to do so. Once I realize what I have done, I may have a number of obligations: to let you know, to apologize, to compensate you if possible. Related actions may be appropriate even if I merely doubt whether I have locked the door. Moreover I might regret my promise, and might inform you of my regrets, either before or after I leave the house. But that doesn't change my commitments and obligations, unless you decide to release me from the promise. None of this amounts to retracting the promise, because promises cannot be unilaterally retracted once accepted.

So if an assertion involves a promise to speak truthfully, then it involves a commitment or undertaking which cannot simply be retracted; the commitment is immediately fulfilled, or not. Nevertheless, we can make sense of the obligations of those who realise they have not spoken truthfully: these are the obligations of compensation and apology owed by someone who realises she has broken a promise. A promise to do something generates an obligation to do that very thing, not an obligation to either do it or else inform, apologize and compensate (this is one respect in which promises seem to differ from contracts). Nevertheless, someone who promises to do something and breaks this promise may thereby acquire obligations to inform, apologize, and compensate.

If I have promised to speak truthfully as to whether *p*, and I realize I have broken this promise, then likewise I am perhaps obliged to let you know that I did not speak truthfully, to apologize, and to compensate you if possible. Some similar actions may be appropriate even if I merely come to doubt whether I have spoken truthfully. This explains why we expect certain behaviours of someone who realizes she asserted a falsehood, even on the assumption that assertion does not involve a commitment to justify what's said.

So my account of assertion in terms of promising to speak truthfully fits into a tradition of understanding assertion as a type of undertaking or commitment, without entailing anything as extensive as Brandom's or MacFarlane's 'commitment' accounts of assertion. Nevertheless, it can help explain why we sometimes feel pressure to justify our assertions, and to apologize when we get things wrong. Moreover, those who still find it plausible that assertion entails commitments to justify could adopt a version of my view according to which assertion involves both promising to speak truthfully and promising to justify (just as my son might promise to complete his homework and also promise to show me the completed homework).

3.4 Promising, Asserting, and Assuring

Assimilation of telling or asserting to promising is often associated with a distinctive 'assurance' view of the epistemic significance of testimony. On such a view, someone's telling me something can give me a distinctive kind of reason to believe it: this is provided by the speaker's assurance, which is understood in terms of the speaker's taking responsibility for the truth of what is said.

In developing his assurance view, Richard Moran (2005) compares promising and assertion without identifying them; for example, he writes of a person 'giv[ing] his word on something to another whether as promise or assertion' (295), referring to 'assurance' in both cases. Moreover Edward S. Hinchman concludes his 'Telling as Inviting to Trust' thus:

> telling is indeed like promising. When I sincerely promise you I'll φ, I intend to make available to you an entitlement to perform acts that rely on taking me at my word. When I sincerely tell you that p, I intend to make available to you an entitlement to believe that p. If each case goes as I intend, in giving you my word I entitle you to take it.   (2005: 587)

This recalls Scanlon:

> When I say 'I promise to be there at ten o'clock to help you,' the effect is the same as if I had said, 'I will be there at ten o'clock to help you. Trust me.'   (1998: 306)

For those who are tempted by the assurance view of testimony, accepting my account of assertion as involving promising to speak truthfully provides a robust framework within which to develop that view. (Still, some caution is advised, given that it is controversial whether promising is primarily aimed at providing assurance.)

But my view does not entail an assurance view of the epistemic significance of testimony, as the situation of eavesdroppers illustrates. Critics of the assurance view (Lackey 2008, Owens 2006, Goldberg 2015) argue that, when I hear you say that p, it makes no epistemic difference whether you are addressing me directly (thus offering me your assurance and inviting me to trust you), or whether I happen to overhear something which was not intended for my ears. Owens remarks that the duty to keep a promise is owed to the promisee in particular, whereas

> By contrast, the kind of epistemic responsibilities at stake in testimony are not duties owed to anyone; testimony can be presented quite unintentionally to an audience who thereby learn that it is true because they are entitled to depend on the speaker for justification.   (117)

On my account, we can acknowledge the special situation of the person who is addressed by the speaker—the person who receives the promise—without insisting that she has some epistemic advantage over the eavesdropper. When an assertion goes wrong—e.g. it is reckless, insincere, or turns out to be false—the person who was addressed seems specially entitled to complain. The eavesdropper lacks such entitlements, even though she may criticize the speaker, just as we criticize people who break their promises to other people. Correspondingly, the responsibility to speak sincerely and competently seems to be owed to the intended audience, rather than to anyone who happened to be passing.

It doesn't follow, however, that the person who was addressed is in a specially advantageous epistemic situation when all goes well. The fact that a speaker is willing to promise to speak truthfully on some matter has the same evidential significance for all concerned, whether addressee or eavesdropper. If such a promise—or any promise—offers something additional and distinctively epistemic to the addressee alone, this needs to be established through further work, and doesn't follow merely from the fact that an assertion involves a promise. It is worth recalling that even Williamson, who is no advocate of assurance accounts, writes of assertion in terms of taking and discharging responsibility:

> To make an assertion is to confer a responsibility (on oneself) for the truth of its content; to satisfy the rule of assertion, by having the requisite knowledge, is to discharge that responsibility, by epistemically ensuring the truth of the content   (2000, 268–9).

So my account of assertion and thus telling or testifying in terms of promising does not commit me to the assurance account of the epistemic value of testimony. However I will return to related issues later on when I discuss trust and trustworthiness in both practical and testimonial situations.

3.5 Alternative Connections

My account allows us to spell out the notion of asserting as incurring responsibility, but without accepting either the 'commitment account' of assertion, or the assurance view of the epistemic significance of testimony. Moreover, it avoids the difficulties encountered by those who have tried to draw analogies between asserting that p and promising that p, as I will now illustrate.

According to Thomas Carson, 'Roughly, a lie is a deliberate false statement that the speaker warrants to be true' (2010: 15). The notion of warrant distinguishes lies from statements made for example in obvious jest, so plays the role given to assertion in other accounts of lying. Carson explicitly connects warranting and promising: 'A warranty of truth is a kind of guarantee or promise that what one says is true.' (25) Carson notes that to make a promise is to place oneself under an obligation to do something, but that

> special problems arise if we attempt to extend this account of promising [to provide] an analysis of warranting the truth of a statement. If one promises to do X, one is placing oneself under an obligation to perform a specific act...However, often when one warrants the truth of a statement, one is not placing oneself under an obligation to perform any particular action or kind of action. (25)

In particular, by warranting that p, one does not become obliged to make it true that p (i.e. to change the world to make it the case that p). Unable to identify a suitable action which is promised in assertion, Carson feels required to treat the notion of warranting the truth of a statement as *sui generis*, rather than as a special case of promising to do something. But if, as I suggest, we see assertion or warranting as involving a promise to speak truthfully (which is simultaneously kept or broken), we have identified a suitable action, without having to associate assertion with obligations of truth-making.

Gary Watson also draws explicit parallels between assertion and promising (2004), arguing that these are different ways of taking responsibility for something, or different ways of warranting. A promise involves a commitment to act as promised, whilst an assertion that p involves commitment to the defensibility of p, where this is weaker than a commitment to defend p if required. Although Watson makes many more interesting points than I can discuss here, it is striking how his distinctions between promises and assertions often depend upon the assumption that if an assertion that p involved a promise, it would either be a promise that p (with attendant puzzles), or else a Brandom-style promise to justify-or-retract p. I am advocating a third—better—way of assimilating assertion to promising.

For example, Watson writes 'Promising itself gives rise to a reason to intend (and do), whereas asserting doesn't create for the asserter a reason to believe what is asserted' (62): this is compatible with the thought that asserting as to whether p creates for the asserter a reason to intend to speak truthfully as to whether p. Or 'In asserting my future intentions, I express my mind; in a promise I commit my mind' (63): again, this distinction can be recognized even if we accept that in asserting my future intentions, I commit to speaking truthfully about my future intentions (there and then).

Assertion is governed by a word-to-world direction of fit. That's to say, we are supposed to adjust our assertions so that they match the world. Promising is governed by a world-to-word direction of fit. That's to say, we are supposed to adjust the world (by acting in it), so that it matches the promises we have made. But when we try to use this distinction in thinking about promises to speak truthfully, we encounter special complexities: adjusting the world here amounts to adjusting what we say. This point holds for situations in which we explicitly promise to speak truthfully, even if I am wrong in claiming that normal assertion involves such a promise.

What then, on my account, is it to promise that p? Suppose Emma says 'I promise that the Moon is smaller than the Earth'. On a deflationary view, Emma makes a sort of heightened assertion that the Moon is smaller than the Earth. It is heightened in the sense that she is governed by especially stringent epistemic norms, or that she is committed to especially grovelling apologies if she gets things wrong. (She is not, of course, promising to make it the case that the Moon is smaller than the Earth). Deflationists might disagree about whether this is really heightened assertion, or just something in the same family as assertion, but the underlying picture is clear.

I endorse this deflationary view of the relationship between promising that p and asserting that p. On my account, then, when Emma says 'I promise that the Moon is smaller than the Earth', she makes an especially solemn, or heightened, promise to speak truthfully as to whether the Moon is smaller than the Earth. The same is true if she says 'I promise that I posted that letter already'. Things get more complex if Emma says 'I promise that I'll come to your party'. There are two ways of reading this: either Emma is making a very firm prediction about her own later state (compare: I promise that I'll have a headache after just one glass of wine), or else she is promising to come to the party. The natural reading is the second, in most contexts.

I have now set out my account of assertion in terms of making and breaking/keeping a promise to speak truthfully. I have distinguished this account from other accounts of assertion in terms of commitment, and from assurance accounts of the epistemic significance of testimony. I have also shown how other authors who have noticed the affinities between assertion and promising have been too quick to set these aside, because of the obvious unattractiveness of identifying an assertion that p with a promise that p.

This means I'm now able to draw on the conclusions of chapter 2, where I argued that promise-making is governed by norms of sincerity and competence. Applying these norms to the special case of promising to speak truthfully helps us understand assertion, and explain our intuitions and disagreements about the norms which govern it.

3.6 Norms on Assertion

I highlighted a sincerity norm, a competence norm, and a norm against promising to act immorally. The last of these raises especially complex issues with regard to speech, which I will discuss later in this chapter. But for the purposes of understanding trust, distrust, and trustworthiness, it is the sincerity and competence norms which are key. Applying these to the case of promising to speak truthfully as to whether p gives the following:

- One must promise to speak truthfully as to whether p only if this promise is sincere
- One must promise to speak truthfully as to whether p only if one is competent to speak truthfully as to whether p.

I will discuss these in turn, before discussing the relationship between norms for promising to speak truthfully and norms for assertion as usually understood.

What is required for sincerity in a promise to speak truthfully as to whether p? Recall the rival suggestions that promises essentially communicate an intention to act or else essentially communicate an intention to become obliged to act. These suggestions return different verdicts in some cases which involve a time-lag between the making of the promise and the keeping-or-breaking of the promise. One might intend to acquire an obligation whilst lacking the intention to meet the obligation, either because one anticipates that acquiring the obligation will generate the appropriate intention, or because one anticipates being released from the obligation before being called upon to act; Owens (2012) can condone such promises as sincere, whilst Scanlon (1998) would not.

But where a promise is simultaneously made and kept-or-broken, there is no space for such cases. Moreover, Owens allows 'that a promise usually carries the implication, or communicates the information that the promisor intends to perform' (2012: 202). So I will assume that one ought to promise to speak truthfully as to whether p only if one intends to speak truthfully as to whether p. Marušić (2015) would argue that sincerity requires us to believe that we will indeed speak truthfully as to whether p. I disagree on this point: this requirement seems to be unduly harsh on hesitant speakers, who do know the truth of what they say, though they have doubts about their ability to express it properly. But this disagreement is not very significant here; at worst, it blurs the distinction between sincerity and competence without undermining the importance of either.

I argued in chapter 2 that good promise-making requires competence: in this instance, do not promise to speak truthfully as to whether p unless you are competent to speak truthfully as to whether p. Keepability is too weak: the mere possibility of speaking truthfully as to whether p does not justify promising to do so. Success here amounts to speaking truthfully, whilst competence involves something like a secure or stable disposition to speak truthfully in this matter.

I am now in a position to make more explicit connections with the standard debate about norms for assertion. If assertion is, as I claim, a matter of promising to speak truthfully as to whether p, and simultaneously keeping or breaking that promise, we should expect it to be governed both by the norms relevant to promise-making and by the norm that promises should be kept. So we'd expect the following:

One must assert as to whether p only if

- One intends to speak truthfully as to whether p
- One is competent to speak truthfully as to whether p
- One does in fact speak truthfully as to whether p.

Distinguishing these various norms makes sense of the range of criticisms to which acts of assertion are prone. Someone who knows whether *p* but intends to deceive may stumble and reveal the truth: she violates the first norm. Someone well-meaning but foolish may accidentally get things right: she violates the second norm. Someone who knows whether *p*, is competent to speak truthfully in this regard, and speaks in good faith may nevertheless stumble and say the wrong thing: she violates the third norm. And of course we may violate more than one norm in a single episode of speech. This multistranded norm recognizes the different ways in which assertions can fall short of the ideal: even imperfect assertions may be satisfactory in certain respects.

Moreover, the distinction between 'objective' and 'subjective' dimensions of assessment—in terms of whether the speaker can reasonably believe herself to satisfy the underlying norm—corresponds to what is called 'primary' and 'secondary' propriety in the literature on assertion:

> While those who assert appropriately (with respect to this rule) in a primary sense will be those who actually obey it, a speaker who broke this rule in a blameless fashion (one who asserted something she didn't know, but reasonably thought she did know) would in some secondary sense be asserting properly.   (DeRose 2002: 180)

DeRose invokes a knowledge rule, but the distinction between primary and secondary propriety generalizes; for example, it is invoked by Weiner (2005) in defence of a truth norm, though Lackey (2008: section 4.5) criticizes this move.

My account of assertion in terms of promising to speak truthfully does not directly commit me to any particular alethic or epistemic norm on assertion, even in conjunction with my earlier account of the norms which govern promise-making (see Maitra (2011) for 'alethic or epistemic'). But it helps us compare, develop, and perhaps vindicate such norms. As illustration, I will briefly survey some proposed norms in the light of this framework.

Williamson (1996, 2000) advocates a knowledge norm of assertion: assert *p* only if you know *p*. Someone who conforms to this rule will at least typically intend to speak truthfully as to whether *p*: an exception would be someone who intends to lie, but accidentally blurts out what she knows, and indeed such an assertion does seem problematic.

Likewise, someone conforming to the knowledge rule is competent to speak truthfully as to whether p, and, moreover, keeps her promise to speak truthfully. (Critics who find the knowledge norm too demanding may argue that knowledge is sufficient but not necessary for competence.)

A side benefit of working with 'asserting as to whether p', as opposed to the standard 'asserting p', is that it becomes easier to separate the sincerity requirement from the knowledge/competence requirement. Williamson's rule that one must know p in order to assert p does of course involve a sincerity requirement, because knowledge involves belief, but this is obscured by the formulation, and by the 'knowledge rule' moniker.

Lackey (2008: 125) advocates the Reasonable To Believe Norm of Assertion:

> One should assert that p only if (i) it is reasonable for one to believe that p, and (ii) if one asserted that p, one would assert that p at least in part because it is reasonable to believe that p.

The RTBNA does not require that the assertor in fact believe that p: Lackey condones 'selfless assertors', such as a creationist teacher who has strong evidence that Homo sapiens evolved from Homo erectus, and asserts this proposition to her pupils, without believing it herself. Plausibly, the creationist teacher is competent to speak truthfully on whether Homo sapiens evolved from Homo erectus, and succeeds in doing so.

Is she sincere? I take it that the teacher does not intend to speak truthfully, but that she does intend to become obliged to speak truthfully: this incurring of unmet obligation is, from her perspective, one downside of her current job. Lackey (2008: 113) says that the assertion is insincere given Bernard Williams's account of insincerity, and yet that the teacher does not aim to misinform her pupils about evolution, seemingly because she aims only to inform her pupils that scientific evidence supports the evolutionary claim. It is not clear to me whether Lackey herself thinks that the assertion is insincere, nor whether she thinks that the teacher intends to misinform her pupils, even if this is not the teacher's aim.

What about Weiner's (2005) truth norm: one must assert p only if p is true? This matches the third strand, the requirement to keep the promise to speak truthfully as to whether p. On this view, the sincerity and competence norms are by-products of the efforts which are required to satisfy the fundamental norm of speaking truthfully. I am not evaluating these rival proposals, but it is worth noting that my account enables us to give appropriate weight to truth in its own right—that's how the promise is kept—whilst enabling us to understand why sincerity and competence have values which are linked to, though not reducible to, the value of truth.

This concludes a non-exhaustive look at some significant philosophical views on the norms of assertion: I have not plumped for one view rather than another, but have instead attempted to show how the considerations which may motivate these different views can be understood and evaluated by accepting that assertion involves promising to speak truthfully.

3.7 Immoral Assertions?

In discussing promise-making, in chapter 2, I identified norms of sincerity and of competence, and along with Altham (1985) and others a requirement that we not promise to do things that are themselves 'wicked' or morally impermissible. How might that third norm apply to the special case of promising to speak truthfully? Under what circumstances could it be immoral to speak truthfully as to whether p? We might think of someone who betrays a secret, utters hurtful truths for fun, or intentionally distracts a bus driver during a tricky manoeuvre. But this is quite a delicate matter. Sometimes it is morally permissible to speak truthfully as to whether p, even though it would be morally impermissible to make a true assertion as to whether p. For example, if you and I have a habit of exchanging jokey insults, I may permissibly say 'your mother never loved you' in a jesting tone—and I know it's true!— but it would be intolerably cruel to assert this.

Can we can make a similarly delicate distinction for other types of promise? Are there instances in which it would be immoral to promise (sincerely, competently) to do something which, considered in itself, is a morally acceptable action? Yes. Suppose we are friends, and you are selling your amateur handicrafts at a charity fundraiser. I purchase various items which I secretly think are too ugly for anyone else to buy: this is a kind gesture which pleases you whilst benefiting the charity, and I manage not to tell any outright lies. But it would be unkind to promise to buy all the too-ugly items, even if you would accede for the charity's sake: making the promise would hurtfully reveal my opinion of the items I subsequently buy. Likewise I shouldn't promise to fix you up a date with my boring cousin, or promise to drive you to your surprise party, at least not in those terms, even though each promised action is perfectly permissible (you're a great match for my hypothetical boring cousin).

When I promise to do something, this can enable others to make reasonable inferences from my subsequent actions to my beliefs, via the assumption that my action is at least partly explained by my desire to keep my promise. And under certain circumstances enabling others to make such inferences is morally impermissible—e.g. it is gratuitously unkind—even though the promised action is itself permissible. (These promises are the mirror image of those discussed by Smith (1997), such as the politician's permissible promise to enact an otherwise-impermissible policy in order to get elected and do much good overall.)

Now, the 'morality' norm on promising which I explored in chapter 2 does not condemn such promises, but this should seem neither surprising nor problematic. We should not expect norms specifically tailored to promise-making to encompass every respect in which an act of promise-making can be assessed: to achieve this, we would need an entire moral theory providing guidance for assessing practical actions of all sorts.

How does this apply to promises to speak truthfully? It can be okay for me to utter a sentence which expresses the claim that your mother never loved you. But if I precede this utterance by promising to speak truthfully, then my utterance takes on a different, crueller, aspect. (Imagine I promise to write something true on a piece of paper, then write 'your mother never loved you' and hand it over.)

So the 'morality' norm on promise-making has limited impact on promising to speak truthfully, forbidding only those promises where merely speaking truthfully would itself be morally problematic, for example where merely voicing a thought can cause the audience to entertain suggestions they would not otherwise have considered. Presenting certain claims in fiction or pretence, or merely as supposition, can sometimes be inflammatory and objectionable, even when it is clear these are not assertions. So promising to speak truthfully in uttering such claims could be forbidden by the norm against promises of immorality. (These remarks presuppose that there are no countervailing considerations: I do not intend to make any contribution here to debates about freedom of expression, nor to suggest that inflammatory fictions are always impermissible.)

3.8 What Sorts of Norms Are These?

I have made constant reference to norms for promise-making, and norms for assertion. But I have not yet discussed whether the latter are constitutive of the practice of assertion, a question which looms large in the literature. Following Williamson (2000: 238), we may compare the practice of assertion to a rule-governed game—the constitutive rules are those which govern the game. One may break the rules and yet play the game, but if one is not sensitive to those rules at all then one is not playing that particular game. In her critical discussion, Maitra (2011: 278) describes constitutive norms as those which one cannot violate 'flagrantly' without ceasing to play the game in question; Rescorla (2009: 101) says that 'a norm is constitutive of a practice iff one must obey the norm to engage correctly in the practice'.

Given the explanatory power of taking assertion to involve both promising to speak truthfully and breaking-or-keeping that promise, it is natural to conclude that this relationship between assertion and promising is itself essential to assertion: if I am right that this relationship holds, then this is simply what it is to make an assertion, rather than something we usually do whilst making an assertion. Then we can ask whether the norms of promise-making which I identified are constitutive of the practice of promising; likewise for the norm of promise-keeping. If so, that would imply that the corresponding norms are constitutive of the practice of assertion, as a special case of promising.

It seems very plausible that if the idea of constitutive norms makes sense at all, then the norm of keeping promises is constitutive of the practice of promising. This is not to say that promises are never broken, but that someone who made no pretence of even attempting to keep their 'promises' could not be sensibly regarded as a promisor. In Rescorla's terms, to engage correctly in the practice of promising one must keep one's promises. Now, I have described this claim as 'very plausible', but a full assessment of the claim would require us to adopt some specific account of the nature and source of promissory obligations. For example, an Owens-style account of promising in terms of our 'authority interest' might make this harder to establish, whilst Rawls (1971: 345) explicitly describes the rule of promise-keeping as a 'constitutive convention', like the rules of a game.

If indeed the norm of keeping promises is constitutive of the practice of promising, then the norm of speaking truthfully is constitutive of the practice of assertion, because assertion involves a promise to speak truthfully. Can we say anything stronger?

Even if we accept that the norm of keeping promises is indeed constitutive of the practice of promising, it is less clear that the norms on promise-making are likewise constitutive. Above, I briefly surveyed how different accounts of promising might explain why promise-making is governed by norms of sincerity and competence in particular. In discussing Rawls on promising, Rescorla says

> He does not mention a constitutive norm against promising to φ when one has no intention of φ-ing, or even when one knows one cannot φ. A natural interpretation, then, is that Rawls does not think insincere promises violate any constitutive norm of promising.   (2009: 107)

Rawls does not endorse insincere promise-making: the point is rather that the norm against insincerity in promise-making is not constitutive of the practice of promising as such, but is an instance of some more general moral norm. Again, establishing whether the norm of sincerity is constitutive of promising would require us to look more closely and carefully at a range of different accounts of the nature of promising (indeed, Rescorla mentions Rawls only to establish the mere coherence of denying that the sincerity norm is constitutive).

So it is less clear whether norms of sincerity and competence are constitutive of promising, and thus constitutive of assertion, as opposed to merely associated with it. Nevertheless, the connection between promising and assertion provides us with another avenue to explore in investigating constitutive norms.

A somewhat different question is what type of normativity is at stake here, and in particular whether these are moral norms. The literature on norms for assertion seems generally to assume that there is no moral issue in play. But false promising and indeed lying are paradigmatically matters of (im)morality. This is a point at which it may make a difference whether we theorize in terms of 'telling' or 'asserting'. Directing our attention to the involvement of an audience makes it easier to recognize the moral dimensions of our practice: both promising and telling are important elements of the ways in which we live together, and they are governed by norms of competence and sincerity. If you lack relevant competence, or you are not recognized as competent by yourself or others, you are distanced from being able to engage properly in these activities. Often we have a moral obligation to be in a certain epistemic state, especially where we have rendered other people dependent upon our competence. I will explore this kind of dependence, and the limitations on what it demands of us, in chapter 4.

I have shown how we can understand assertion as involving a promise which is immediately kept or broken; this enables us to vindicate the thought that assertion and promising are importantly similar, without implausibly identifying asserting that p with promising that p. Moreover, we can adopt this view without thereby adopting either a 'commitment account' of assertion or an assurance account of the epistemic significance of testimony, though it is compatible with such accounts. Finally, I have argued that promising is governed by a competence (or perhaps success) norm, and that this, in combination with the view of assertion as involving promising to speak truthfully, explains the structure of debate around norms for assertion. Having examined both promising and asserting as ways of incurring commitment, I now turn to questions of trustworthiness.

Additional Sources

3.1 Telling and Asserting. Hornsby (1994) and E. Fricker (2006) explicitly work with 'telling', though their primary interests differ from one another. Heal (2013) also writes of 'telling', with very helpful distinctions between types of telling. 'Assertion' is both the title and the core term throughout the various essays in Brown and Cappelen (eds) (2011) and in Goldberg's monograph (2015), although Goldberg also discusses telling. Kukla (2014) emphasizes the audience's role in determining whether an utterance is an assertion, and I draw on her work through chapters 5 and 6.

3.2 Connecting Asserting with Promising. Watson (2004) is a key discussion of the seeming differences between assertion and telling; likewise Owens (2006). My neutral use of 'speaking' is much like Cappelen (2011: 22–4) on 'saying'; again, verbal utterances are standing in for writing, signing (e.g. ASL, BSL), Morse code, semaphore, etc. It's not obvious how far this list could be extended.

3.3 Asserting and Committing. References to Brandom and Macfarlane are given in the text.

3.4 Promising, Asserting, and Assuring. A different, rewarding treatment of assurance, in connection with J. L. Austin, is given by Lawlor (2013).

3.5 Alternative Connections. Williamson (2000: 244–5) discusses swearing that p.

3.6 Norms on Assertion. In addition to citations in the main text, the essays in part 2 of Brown and Cappelen (eds) (2011) cover a lot of relevant ground.

3.7 Immoral Assertions? A much richer set of discussions of speech and ethics is gathered in Maitra and McGowan (eds) 2012. I take up on some related questions around coercion and lies in my (2018a).

3.8 What Sorts of Norms Are These? Key references are in the main text.

4

Trustworthiness

In my opening chapter, I proposed an account of trust and distrust in terms of commitment. In chapters 2 and 3 I focused on two prominent ways in which we explicitly take on new commitments, through promising, and through assertion; I argued that assertion involves promise-making. Such commitments should not be incurred unless the person in question is both competent to fulfil the commitment and sincere in taking it on.

Paradigm cases of promising and assertion are voluntary and explicit: we imagine the speaker as saying 'I promise…', or as clearly and seriously articulating the proposition asserted. But in practice we often acquire commitments in much less clear-cut ways, for example by nodding, by failing to object to suggestions or presuppositions, by allowing others to continue in their expectations of us, or by receiving a favour within a social practice of reciprocity. This inevitable lack of clarity means that we are often mistaken about what commitments we have, or about what commitments those around us have, and indeed about what we and others know about our own commitments. These are familiar phenomena which create difficulties and drama in our ordinary interactions, at home, at work, and in public life; I will explore some of these difficulties and dramas in chapters 5 and 6.

I won't offer a detailed theory of how commitments are incurred: in large part this will be an empirical question, one which is answered differently in different social contexts. Nevertheless, I plan to explore the notions of trust, distrust, and trustworthiness which are tied to commitment-fulfilment, in ways which go beyond the more explicit cases of promise-making and assertion discussed in earlier chapters. Even though the boundaries are fuzzy, it is obvious that we are deeply involved in non-explicit practices of commitment: imagine how much of our everyday social life would crumble if people insisted upon fulfilling only

How To Be Trustworthy. Katherine Hawley, Oxford University Press (2019). © Katherine Hawley.
DOI: 10.1093/oso/9780198843900.001.0001

those commitments they had explicitly signed up to. Disingenuousness on this front can make someone maddening to deal with, either in person or as a political figure. And in my view these practices of non-explicit commitment are tied up with issues of trust, distrust, and trustworthiness of the same general kind as those concerning explicit promise and assertion.

In this chapter, I explore trustworthiness in the context of the commitment account of trust and distrust, articulating a rather negative account of trustworthiness, in terms of avoiding unfulfilled commitment. Untrustworthiness can be a matter of deceit or malicious intentions; but equally, I will argue, it can arise from well-intentioned over-commitment, from allowing our commitments to outstrip our ability to meet those commitments. As I will show, the pursuit of trustworthiness is compatible with some neglect of other virtues, values and goals. Indeed, it sometimes requires us to neglect those other aspects of life, for better or for worse.

4.1 Trustworthiness and Commitment

I began the book with trust and distrust. But trustworthiness and untrustworthiness often seem more central to moral philosophy than do trust and distrust themselves. Trust sometimes has value in its own right, but usually this is conditional on the trustworthiness of the trusted person. As Linda Zagzebski puts it, the virtue of trust is 'a mean between gullibility and suspiciousness' (1996, 160–1): virtue involves wise trusting and distrusting, not trust per se. We owe it to ourselves and to others to place our trust appropriately, where appropriateness depends at least in part on the trustworthiness of the trustee. This is especially important where we make decisions about trust which in turn affect people who depend upon us, whether these are our children, colleagues, friends, or neighbours.

Different notions of trust and distrust correspond to different notions of trustworthiness and untrustworthiness. Given the commitment account, to be trustworthy is to ensure that our commitments are matched by action, and thus, as a special case, to ensure that what we say in making an assertion is true. This requires diligence in fulfilling commitments already acquired—a trustworthy person keeps her promises. But it also requires judiciousness in the acquisition of new commitments: trustworthy people must sometimes disappoint up-front by refusing new commitments, rather than violate trust later on. Likewise, when we are asked for information we do not have, 'no comment' may be a disappointing response, yet it can reflect greater trustworthiness than an ill-founded assertion would.

On this view, trustworthiness is above all a matter of avoiding untrustworthiness, by following through on existing commitments, but also by avoiding certain commitments in the first place. In this sense, it is a negative account: trustworthiness does not require us to take on as many commitments as we can manage, or to make certain commitments rather than others, except where these follow from our existing commitments. It only requires us to avoid unfulfilled commitments. I will explore the ramifications of this idea at some length below. But at this point I want to offer some motivation for taking this kind of negative picture seriously.

One motivation is that this account of trustworthiness is the flipside of the account of trust and distrust which I advocated in chapter 1: if such an account of trust and distrust is worth taking seriously, then so too is the corresponding account of trustworthiness. In addition, thinking about trustworthiness provides further reasons to reject alternative accounts of trust and distrust.

For example, accounts which understand trust as imputing a certain kind of motive to the trusted person do not straightforwardly generate an account of what trustworthiness in general requires. Someone merits your trust on a particular occasion, on such a view, if they are motivated, in the right way, to act as you prefer or need. But this cannot generalize: if trustworthiness is thought of as a kind of well-meaning helpfulness, it will always be possible for us to subjugate more of our own interests to those of others, demonstrating more goodwill, competence, and responsiveness. We will be pulled in different directions by the whims of those around us, unable to be trustworthy to all. Worse, if trustworthiness were a generalized tendency to respond to people's trust, rather than to their interests or needs, then it would be relatively easy for distrusted people to be trustworthy, since they have little trust to respond to.

Moreover trustworthiness cannot in general be a matter of responding to others' normative expectations, because such expectations may be unreasonable, and defying unreasonable expectations is not a sign of untrustworthiness. Trustworthiness involves responding to reasonable or appropriate normative expectations, but this returns us to the question of what makes such expectations appropriate.

Thinking in terms of commitment reminds us that other people's expectations are sometimes unreasonable, and that trustworthiness does not require us to respond to all the needs or wishes of those around us. A trustworthy person may appear to be untrustworthy, if others are mistaken about what commitments she has incurred. Anticipation of this kind of misunderstanding may lead a trustworthy person to behave as other people expect her to do, either for their sake or for the sake of preserving her own reputation. But this does not entail that trustworthiness requires her to act in such ways; I explore related issues in section 4.6, and in chapter 6.

Moreover, thinking in terms of commitment allows us to build an account of general trust, not tied to any specific task. We can understand general trust as reliance on someone to fulfil whatever commitments she may have, and general distrust as lack of such reliance. Most trust is intermediate between the specific and the completely general: I may trust someone to fulfil her financial commitments, without trusting her to fulfil commitments in her personal life. This kind of differentiation is entirely normal, especially when we bear in mind that untrustworthiness can derive from incompetence or misjudgement, not just from ill will: most of us are incompetent and prone to misjudgement in certain areas of life, without being all-round hopeless cases.

Understanding trustworthiness in terms of commitment enables us to give a satisfying account of both trust and distrust, including an account of what those attitudes target, and when they are appropriate. Thinking of trustworthiness in terms of commitment allows space for a coherent picture of trustworthiness as something which can be aspired to in ourselves or demanded of others.

This somewhat thin, quasi-contractual notion of trustworthiness can seem inadequate to the complexities of intimate relationships, where we hope for and expect much more than this sort of scrupulousness about promise-keeping and caution around commitment. I entirely agree that often we are required to do much more than merely avoid unfulfilled commitments, both within intimate relationships and more generally. However, as I explore below, doing much more can be in tension with the goal of avoiding unfulfilled commitments; this may be especially common when we are in challenging circumstances, cornered into making tricky but significant choices about what to prioritize.

It is exactly because I want to explore this tension that it is vital for me to hold onto the somewhat thin, negative notion of trustworthiness I am developing here, rather than expanding it to include additional demands. I think there are plenty of good reasons for using the term 'trustworthiness' for the somewhat thin notion, but if that still jars, you are of course free to think of 'avoiding unfulfilled commitment' in its place where necessary. This is certainly an ethically and socially important notion, worthy of study even if you doubt whether it is a central notion of trustworthiness.

What is the role of motive in this account of trustworthiness? I have already argued that trustworthiness cannot require us to be constantly motivated by others' needs and desires. But does it require us to be motivated by our commitments? According to the commitment account, you can trust someone to do something without expecting her to be motivated by her commitment. You may trust me to do something because you believe both that I have a commitment to do it, and that I will do it, without believing that I will do it because of my commitment. Maybe I am motivated by pure enthusiasm. Would commitment have motivated me in the counterfactual absence of enthusiasm? Perhaps then there would have been no commitment: this needn't indicate that I am untrustworthy. One way of becoming more trustworthy is by trying to restrict one's commitments—so far as possible—to those which one can enthusiastically fulfil.

To be trustworthy in some specific respect, on this view, it is enough to behave in accordance with one's commitment, regardless of motive. What about general trustworthiness? In practice, sadly, none of us has independent reasons to do all the things we are committed to doing. So general trustworthiness encompasses more than the fair-weather cases in which we don't need the motivation of commitment: a generally trustworthy person will often meet her commitments simply because they are her commitments, although this is not a requirement of trustworthiness in any specific respect. (My neglect of motive is one of several reasons why this account of trustworthiness does not sit comfortably within a virtue ethical approach.)

So a trustworthy person is good at managing her commitments: she will take care not to over-commit, to ensure that she can fulfil the commitments she does undertake. But commitments are not always under our immediate control, and in particular we can find ourselves with commitments arising from others' continuing and acknowledged expectations, or indeed from our own prior commitments.

For example, in the context of ongoing relationships—whether these are in the workplace, within the family, or amongst friends—an earlier commitment to engaging in a relationship or practice may often involve an implicit commitment to take on further, more specific commitments in future. If we are friends, then I am not free to turn down an invitation to your birthday party without a very good reason. This is not because I am already committed to attending your birthday party before you invite me. After all, it is easier for me to decline the invitation than it is for me to skip the party once I have accepted the invitation: that's to say, I need a smaller excuse in the former case than in the latter. Nevertheless, as your friend it is harder for me to turn down the invitation than it would be for a mere acquaintance who could acceptably say, for example, that she's just not fond of parties. Likewise in some types of professional job, an employee is contracted to accept work, take on projects, and so on, but with a degree of flexibility which allows her some freedom to choose which projects to adopt, so long as the overall quantity and quality is acceptable, and high-level goals are met. That is, by signing the initial contract, the employee is committed to taking on later, more specific commitments, but she does not thereby immediately take on a particular set of later commitments rather than some other set. This kind of flexibility is one of the privileges of much professional work, but it has its limits.

For ease of discussion, I will sometimes refer to these commitments-to-take-on-commitments as 'meta-commitments': they vary in strength and explicitness, and disagreements about these can be the source of deep problems in relationships, around mismatch of expectations. If you think that a friend needs a very good reason not to accept an invitation to take a vacation together, and I think that friends are free to choose whether or not to vacation together, then that will be a source of difficulty for our friendship when I turn down your kind invitation to join you in Blackpool. Fulfilment of meta-commitments may often be what is at stake when we think of simply trusting someone, rather than trusting someone to do something specific. More generally, loyalty often involves a kind of meta-commitment, but one which may be understood very differently by different people; I will return in chapter 5 to discuss questions around how we identify commitments, in ourselves and others.

In discussing trust (chapter 1), I insisted upon the importance of also keeping distrust in focus. What about untrustworthiness? In effect, I am treating trustworthiness as a matter of avoiding untrustworthiness—i.e. avoiding unfulfilled commitment by whatever means. But we might wonder whether there are situations in which neither label is appropriate, and not just because a person is hovering around the border between trustworthiness and untrustworthiness, by being somewhat trustworthy and somewhat untrustworthy. For example, a hermit who has no commitments whatsoever easily manages to avoid unfulfilled commitments; we might be reluctant to describe hermits either as trustworthy or as untrustworthy. Moreover inanimate objects and babies lack unfulfilled commitments, because they lack commitments. Yet we don't call them 'trustworthy'.

Since I want to retain the connection between trust, distrust, trustworthiness, and commitment, I have three main options here. The first is to rule that trustworthiness requires at least a few fulfilled commitments, alongside a lack of unfulfilled commitments, and to note that hermits, babies, and inanimate objects do not satisfy this requirement. The second is to rule that trustworthiness requires a disposition to fulfil commitments once incurred, then argue that neither babies nor inanimate objects have such a disposition, whilst a hermit might possess or lack such a disposition. In practice, these two options blur into one another, since presumably we can acquire a disposition to fulfil commitments only through experience of making, breaking, and keeping commitments. Even the hermit once lived in a family or broader society; if not, he would be more like a baby or an animal, incapable of undertaking commitment rather than merely able to avoid doing so.

If we are to choose between these, then the second, dispositional option seems preferable. It avoids awkward questions about exactly how few commitments one needs to have fulfilled (and how recently) in order to count as trustworthy. More importantly, it fits with the ways in which we attribute trustworthiness when thinking about who to ask for information, or for a favour. We often want to know whether someone would fulfil a commitment if she were to take it on; information about past performance can be good evidence in this regard, but is not the whole story.

But the third option is to dodge this issue. My main goals are to explore the ways in which, in the course of our ordinary social existences, the pursuit of trustworthiness can conflict with other important goals or values, and to explore how circumstances can help or hinder us in trying to strike an appropriate balance. These issues arise for all of us who are not complete hermits; in fact the 'ornamental' hermits of eighteenth-century follies were very much embedded into social structures, even if they had little direct contact with other people.

In my discussion of trust and distrust I made a great fuss about cases in which neither trust nor distrust was appropriate, whereas here I am recommending we make little fuss about cases in which neither trust-worthiness nor untrustworthiness seems to be a suitable category. Am I being consistent? I believe so. Recognizing that many interactions fall outside the scope of trust and distrust is crucial to ordinary social rela-tions: even in the most intimate relationships, it's important that not everything be done through commitment and obligation. We also need space for self-concern, supererogation, surprises, and casual gestures. Such situations are central to our thinking about trust and distrust, whilst hermits and babies are not central to our thinking about trustworthiness and untrustworthiness.

4.2 Trustworthiness Beyond Sincerity

Once a commitment has been incurred, trustworthiness requires both good intentions and competence. Correspondingly, untrustworthiness can arise when commitment is not matched by good intentions, and it can arise when commitment is not matched by competence; these fail-ings are often intertwined.

Although there is room for dispute about exactly what intention (or other mental state) is required in order to make a sincere promise (chapter 2), for most purposes we can assume that a sincere promise is one which is backed by an intention to act as promised. Moreover

I argued that making an assertion on some matter involves making a promise to speak truthfully regarding that matter, and either keeping or breaking that promise. Trustworthiness requires us not to make commitments where we will lack the intention to live up to the commitment—i.e. to keep the promise by speaking truthfully. This means that mere lack of appropriate intention is a form of untrustworthiness: one can be untrustworthy without positively intending to break a promise one has made. Thus bullshit, in Harry Frankfurt's sense (2005)—speech which is unconstrained by regard for either truth or falsity—exemplifies untrustworthiness, since the speaker doesn't positively intend to speak truthfully. Likewise, someone who makes a promise for immediate gain, without any regard to whether she will keep the promise, displays untrustworthiness.

Trustworthiness does not require us already to have the intention to fulfil a commitment before incurring it: often we foresee that promising to do something will induce in us an intention to do that thing, and indeed that's sometimes why we make promises, as a form of indirect self-control. (Perhaps trustworthiness does require us to have a general intention to fulfil commitments, whatever they may turn out to be, or a conditional intention to do things if we are committed to doing them.) For this reason, the requirement is that we avoid having commitments which are not matched by appropriate intentions; we can achieve this in part by predicting whether certain commitments will give rise to the right intentions.

But even with these details spelt out, it is plain that good intentions are not enough. I have already made the case for a competence requirement both in connection with promising and in connection with assertion or telling (chapters 2 and 3). But it is also possible to see the direct connection with trustworthiness and the value thereof. Someone who regularly takes on too much and ends up letting people down, even to her evident dismay, is an untrustworthy person. She is unreliable, and where this is a pattern there is no reason to deny that it is a form of untrustworthiness; it is certainly a form of behaviour that, over time, will lead her to be distrusted by others, and rightly so. This sort of incompetence can involve taking on commitments which are individually too challenging, or it can involve taking on commitments which are individually quite manageable, but collectively overwhelming.

When I discuss these ideas with others, I find that some are reluctant to describe this sort of person as 'untrustworthy', preferring to reserve that term for those who are dishonest, insincere, or intentionally manipulative. (Uncoincidentally, most of us regard ourselves as more inclined to this kind of well-intentioned over-commitment than to outright deception; I include myself here of course.) Isn't incompetence in these respects just a matter of unreliability, rather than untrustworthiness? As I discussed in chapter 1, ordinary language is not a consistent guide in this area, and I do not want to linger long over the choice of terminology. But what is important is that untrustworthiness-through-incompetence can have much of the same ethical and practical character as does untrustworthiness-through-bad-intentions. Indeed, we often find it difficult to decide whether someone really isn't able to fulfil her commitments, or whether she just isn't willing to do so. This uncertainty can also arise in the first person, of course, when I wonder whether I am really trying my best to live up to my commitments.

If this seems a stretch, it may be because we can easily imagine or remember cases in which someone over-commits without realizing that she is taking on too much—which may make her seem less blameworthy—whereas it is perhaps harder to imagine a case in which someone does not realize she is being insincere in her assertions or promises. I'll return later to discuss whether trustworthiness requires just competence or also knowledge of competence, and also to explore the nature and consequences of commitment without proper competence. But already it should be clear that not knowing that one is over-committed will not serve as an all-purpose excuse for failure, nor as a mark of trustworthiness.

It is a familiar thought that lies and false promises are morally wrong, exceptional circumstances aside. And it might seem harsh to suggest that incompetence or ignorance is likewise a moral flaw. It is certainly not in general a moral flaw to lack competence or be ignorant: we are all inevitably multi-incompetent and multi-ignorant. Nor even is it in general a moral flaw to lack competence which others want or need you to possess. But recall that, on my view, trustworthiness requires competence only insofar as we have commitments. And it is morally problematic to end up in a situation in which you are committed to doing something you are not competent to do, absent a good excuse at least.

A misleading shorthand for what I want to say is that trustworthiness requires competence. It is misleading because one can be trustworthy even whilst having very little competence or knowledge, so long as one avoids commitments which would require such competence or knowledge. The less misleading formulation is to say that trustworthiness requires us to undertake commitments only where we have the competence to fulfil those commitments. We sometimes have control over which commitments we take on. And we sometimes have control over what competence we have, both in the sense that we can learn new skills but also in the sense that we can adapt our circumstances, not least through managing what commitments we take on. Thus there can be more than one way of achieving trustworthiness in a certain domain, compatible with greater and lesser degrees of competence and commitment, so long as the latter is not allowed to outstrip the former.

Still, I haven't given you an account of what competence really is or requires, and I am not going to do so. In some contexts, the notion of competence may seem closer to true belief than to knowledge, closer to a reliable capacity for successful action than to know-how (for those who wish to make that distinction). In effect, I was exploring these possibilities in discussing the various possible competence norms in chapters 2 and 3. This distances me from others who have written about epistemic norms for action, for assertion, and the like, since I am not concerned to make the fine distinctions which preoccupy them. This is because, as we will see later, the practical issues rarely seem to hang on those distinctions, even though the distinctions may be of interest in their own right. The main point about competence that I will carry forward, in addition to its contrast with sincerity, is that what we are competent to do can depend in important, constitutive ways on the material and social circumstances we find ourselves in, as I will explain below.

4.3 What Trustworthiness Permits

I have emphasized that a trustworthy person must sometimes disappoint people by refusing to take on commitments which she will not or cannot fulfil: trustworthiness sometimes requires us to act contrary to other people's hopes or wishes. This is in part an issue of demandingness: most of us are embedded in such a rich network of people with so many needs and desires that we cannot consistently respond to all of these. Trustworthiness does not require us to minimize our social contacts in the light of human neediness. What is perhaps more surprising is not just that trustworthiness permits us to avoid unreasonable demands, but that it permits us to avoid even quite reasonable demands.

Trustworthiness requires that our commitments not outstrip our actions; it does not require us to extend our commitments as far as possible within that constraint. A trustworthy person may disappoint people up-front for no good reason at all, even though she knows that if she took on the commitment she would be willing and able to follow through. So one strategy for achieving trustworthiness is to be very reluctant to take on new commitments: there is a wide range of possible commitment-levels which are all compatible with trustworthiness. You will recognize this variety if you think about your friends, colleagues, family members, and neighbours, and about yourself. After all, being trustworthy isn't everything: some people are highly trustworthy whilst being rather ungenerous. Conversely, generous, charitable, or simply enthusiastic impulses easily coexist with untrustworthiness, at least where untrust-worthiness arises from lack of competence rather than lack of goodwill.

Why do we sometimes resist taking on commitments even when we could easily fulfil them? Often of course it's because we just don't want to do the thing in question, and realize that if we take on the commitment we will face an unhappy choice between doing what we prefer to avoid, or else violating norms, with foreseeable social consequences. But some-times we may be indifferent to the action, or positively intend to do it, yet prefer to act outside the framework of commitment and duty. Why have this preference?

One reason is that avoiding commitment allows us flexibility, in case we change our minds or something else comes up. In the case of speech, where there is no time delay between incurring the commitment and fulfilling (or failing to fulfil) it, the corresponding urge is to absolve one-self from responsibility for the truth of what is said, even whilst saying it; often we'd like to maintain plausible deniability.

Sometimes there are less sinister reasons for preferring to act outside of commitment and duty: for example, there can be good, altruistic reasons for not wanting to offer someone an epistemic assurance of your future action (or the truth of what you say), even when you yourself possess such assurance. You may be trying to teach someone how to be independent, to wean someone off a habit of relying upon you; parents are often in this situation. Moreover, there is no point promising someone that you will throw them a surprise party on their birthday. And, more self-servingly, we may like the fact that people are often more grateful, or express their gratitude differently, when we act without being obliged to do so. On the other hand, people are often grateful for assurance, so this isn't a straightforward calculation.

Doesn't trustworthiness require us to take on new commitments? As I discussed above, often we incur meta-commitments, whereby we undertake to be open to future additional commitments without actually incurring them ahead of time. This means that on occasion trustworthiness will indeed require us to take on new commitments, as we have undertaken to do. But where meta-commitments do not bind us, attention to trustworthiness leaves us free to reduce our burden of commitment quite substantially. This is another reason why I have tried not to refer to trustworthiness as a 'virtue': on one standard philosophical account of the virtues, they are mutually reinforcing, and indeed cannot be fully achieved independently. The valuable trait of trustworthiness which I am exploring here does not have that kind of relationship to other valuable traits such as generosity or kindness.

4.4 What Attention to Trustworthiness Can Require

I have argued that trustworthiness is compatible with a wide range of degrees of commitment and that, even though the pursuit of other positive traits, values, and goals may require us to take on commitments sometimes, one can be trustworthy without doing so. Indeed, this was built into the way I set things up in chapter 1, when I argued that we should not identify the attitude of trust with relying upon others to meet their obligations, exactly because trustworthiness is a somewhat richer trait than the all-purpose virtue of meeting one's obligations. Being trustworthy is compatible with falling short in other ways, both with respect to other people and with respect to our own personal flourishing.

We are now in a position to recognize something a little stronger and stranger. Concern with our own trustworthiness permits us to neglect other important goals. But in addition it can sometimes require us to neglect other important goals. A concern for trustworthiness can be in tension with values such as generosity or enthusiasm, and it can be in tension with the aspiration to gain new competences. It can lead us to miss out on important opportunities by making us cautious about taking on commitments, even when we positively value traits like generosity and kindness, or the practical and intrinsic advantages of collaborating with others socially.

There is a weaker and a stronger version of this point. The weaker version is that we can't do everything we would like to do for ourselves or others, and so we shouldn't commit to doing everything we would like to do. In particular, it is unsurprising if a generous impulse or a flash of enthusiasm tempts us to make a commitment we would not be competent to fulfil, and unsurprising that we can feel disappointed when we realize that the trustworthy response is to resist this temptation, even in the face of others' wishes. This is another way of seeing that untrustworthiness can sometimes flow from admirable motives: often we want to commit to helping others, or to doing things which would be intrinsically valuable, even though taking on such a commitment would violate the competence norm.

In itself, this doesn't generate a genuine conflict between what trustworthiness demands and what, for example, generosity requires, even though in such cases we may feel a generous urge pulling us in one direction, and an urge to trustworthiness pulling in the opposite direction. This isn't yet a genuine conflict because, I take it, it's not genuinely generous to make a commitment we're not competent to keep, even when the temptation to do so flows from a generous nature.

The stronger version of the point relies on the fact that often we cannot easily tell what competencies we possess, for all sorts of reasons. What we are competent to do depends on complex facts about the future, and about our physical and social environment, as well as our intrinsic abilities or strengths. We don't always know what we can do, and we don't always know what a given commitment will demand of us. (It's also true that we don't always know whether we have a certain commitment, and that we don't always know whether we are sincere: I discuss this in chapter 5.) There are plenty of situations in which we are in fact competent to keep a certain commitment, but do not know that we are; likewise, there are situations in which we justifiably believe that we are competent, though in fact we are not.

This means that if I make commitments only when I know that I am competent to fulfil them, then I will miss out on a range of commitments I might otherwise have made, for the sake of others or myself, and which I am in fact competent to fulfil. In such situations, concern with my own trustworthiness is in direct tension with other values. That's because, when caution prevents me from making a commitment to act generously, one that I am in fact competent to fulfil, it doesn't seem that I am being generous all things considered. This is the key contrast between the weaker version of the point and the stronger version I am now considering.

For most norms, we can distinguish between satisfying the norm and knowing (or reasonably believing) that you are satisfying the norm: you can follow a rule without knowing that you are doing so, and you can break a rule without knowing that you are doing so. Typically we rely upon this sort of distinction in thinking about blame for norm violations. But I want to avoid engaging too much with general considerations about norms, blame, and transparency. Instead, I'm trying to outline a framework which will help us understand a range of problems, dilemmas, misunderstandings, and injustices we encounter in everyday life when judging trustworthiness in ourselves and others. So here are some points intended to be useful for that purpose; these provide a first take on some issues I explore more carefully in chapter 5 and 6.

One common situation is this: I lack perfect insight into my own competence (of course), but am nevertheless considering taking on a new commitment which would require a particular competence. I wonder whether I will be able to manage this commitment properly. People handle such decisions with varying degrees of caution, and both extremes seem problematic.

Suppose I am very reluctant to take on the commitment, because of a small degree of uncertainty about my ability to fulfil it. Such extreme caution can look very much like self-centredness masquerading as heartfelt concern not to let other people down. If the preservation of my own honour and clean hands is always foremost in my mind, then I have things out of balance, to put it mildly. This is the kind of situation invoked by pejorative terms such as 'fastidious', 'fussy', 'over-concern', or even 'caution', and it is the kind of situation in which it is difficult to develop good working or personal relationships.

This is an unsympathetic portrayal of the reasons for being over-cautious about taking on new commitments. But some people may be exceptionally cautious in this way for more sympathetic reasons, including a quasi-pathological lack of self-confidence, or an awareness of the high personal costs they will have to pay if they erroneously become over-committed. Moreover, the language of fussiness can be used to bully others into taking on what are in fact genuinely unwise commitments. But this reinforces my point that it's possible to be over-cautious in taking on commitment: this is why even a false accusation of over-caution has some bite.

There is a risk of undermining relationships by saying 'no' to other people too often. Indeed, people usually want us to say 'yes', not just 'I'll do my best'. In the context of testimony or information-provision, people like us to assert outright, rather than constantly hedging with 'as far as I know...', 'well it seems quite likely that...' and so on. If we focus upon trustworthiness alone, this can seem puzzling: why not admire such caution? The reason is that we collectively value other traits in addition to trustworthiness, and paying undue special attention to trustworthiness can pull against the development of those other values.

Contrasting with over-caution, the other extreme is a kind of recklessness in commitment-making. This occurs when people take on commitments despite having very little evidence that they are competent to fulfil the commitment, or perhaps without having properly considered whatever evidence may be available. Imagine that I barely pause to think about whether I'll be able to act in line with a commitment, and just jump straight in. Exactly how we characterize what's wrong here may depend on our broader views in ethics and epistemology. There are a range of distinctions we can make, using terminology such as 'knowledge', 'reasonable', 'justification', and so on. But not much will depend on this in the chapters to come, so although these distinctions are interesting in their own right, I will not pause over them here. What's essential is only that we recognize that trustworthiness is sometimes incompatible with rushing thoughtlessly into taking on demanding commitments.

Between these two extremes, there is a range of approaches and seemingly no single most appropriate degree of epistemic caution to exercise in taking on commitments. This means that in many ordinary situations involving uncertainty we will be pulled one way by attention to trustworthiness, and simultaneously pulled another way by attention to other values and goals; there will be no mechanical way of resolving such tensions.

As I discussed briefly above, there can be other reasons for withholding commitment, not just careful attention to the demands of trustworthiness. In particular, we can be over-committed even when we are capable of meeting all our commitments, in the sense that we may have so many commitments to others that we are left unable to pursue those projects which make our own lives meaningful. And even in the closest of relationships it is important to carve out areas of thought, speech, and action which are not governed by commitment and obligation. Nevertheless, my focus will be on the ways in which diligence about trustworthiness, and consequent caution about commitment, can point away from other valuable features of life. This is a useful lens through which to see a variety of practical problems in self-management and interaction with others.

4.5 Assertion and Telling

As explained in chapter 3, I am treating telling or asserting as involving promise-like commitment to speak truthfully there and then. I think that this treatment has many merits, but of particular importance to my overall project is that it makes possible a unified account of trust, distrust, trustworthiness, and untrustworthiness across the domains of action and speech. In this chapter so far I have focused on trustworthiness in connection with commitments to practical action; but the issues I have discussed have direct analogues when we think about trustworthiness in testimony.

Trustworthiness requires us not to over-reach in terms of our assertions; this point, in somewhat different guise, is familiar from debates around epistemic norms for assertion. Competence in this realm is competence to speak truthfully on the matter at hand. However, trustworthiness is compatible with saying relatively little, or at least asserting relatively little, either by remaining silent or by speaking in a hedging or speculative fashion which tries to evade responsibility for the truth of what is said. That is, we may avoid any attempt to speak truthfully, or we may attempt to speak truthfully but without framing this as fulfilment of a commitment to do so. This reflects my understanding of trustworthiness as a primarily negative requirement to avoid unfulfilled commitments, rather than a positive requirement to seek out new commitments and fulfil them.

In the case of practical action, there can be many reasons to take on new commitments: generosity, kindness, enthusiasm, self-promotion, or a sense of duty. Likewise, there can be many reasons to make an assertion, to volunteer information: it's often helpful to others, it can be fun, it can be rude not to, it can deepen relationships, promote the speaker's interests, and so on. But these are not in general reasons which directly derive from the pursuit of trustworthiness, as distinct from the desire to demonstrate trustworthiness. An exception concerns 'meta-commitments', where we incur commitments to be open to later, non-specific commitments. There are meta-commitments with respect to assertion: things we say, roles we accept, or relationships we enter into may commit us to later volunteering whatever information we may have, or to speaking out in various situations.

So, setting these meta-commitments aside, trustworthiness often permits us to be sparing with our assertions. Moreover, a concern with trustworthiness can drive us towards caution in this respect, and sometimes to go too far with our caution. Just as we can become overly fastidious with regard to practical commitment, over-concern with trustworthiness can turn us into unhelpful speakers, thereby damaging ourselves and others. Unhelpfulness here needn't involve remaining silent, but can include hedging formulations such as 'I believe that...', 'last time I checked...' or 'it seems pretty likely that...'. Hedging is in some sense a safer option for those who are concerned to maintain their own trustworthiness, even at the cost of other values.

Why don't we always take this safer option? After all, if I believe something, typically I can be more certain that I have this belief than that the belief itself is true. So why not just say that I believe it, rather than committing to the truth of the claim itself? In practice, such hedged assertions are not merely weaker than they could be, they are often actively misleading for exactly this reason, as explained by Paul

Grice's Co-operative Principle. The Principle enjoins you to 'Make your conversational contribution such as is required, at the stage at which it occurs, by the accepted purpose or direction of the talk exchange in which you are engaged.' (1989: 26) A further maxim, that of informativeness, means if we make a hedged claim we imply that this is the strongest, most informative claim available to us, which is misleading if we are simply being overcautious.

Beyond this specific issue about hedging, the theme of conversational cooperation raises numerous questions in connection with commitment and trustworthiness. Does becoming engaged in conversation generate a kind of meta-commitment, pushing us to take on later commitments that would be useful to our interlocutor or which would otherwise advance the conversation? At the very least, many of us can recognize a feeling of reluctance to engage someone in conversation unless either we're happy to continue indefinitely or else we know that some external event will soon bring the conversation to an end. (Or perhaps that's a peculiarly British problem.)

Conversational cooperativeness can pull in the opposite direction to trustworthiness, making us over-eager to contribute in potentially unsafe ways. But it's not hard to see that if we focus on resisting this temptation, becoming overcautious about our commitments, then we risk irritating those around us. In leaving the audience to make up its own mind, instead of providing assurance for them, we may seem concerned primarily to avoid recrimination. Clean hands and plausible deniability again spring to mind. Focused concern on trustworthiness can lead people to become unhelpfully cautious testifiers, and indeed bad teachers. But undue lack of concern about trustworthiness also makes us bad testifiers, liable to assert what is not true. As in the practical realm, there is no mechanical method for deciding what policy to adopt, or what to say (or not) in any particular situation.

4.6 Trustworthiness and Perceived Trustworthiness

I have argued that the pursuit of trustworthiness permits, indeed sometimes requires, turning away from other important values and goals (or at least that there is an important, central notion of trustworthiness for which this is true). This is supported by the claim that trustworthiness does not direct us to take on specific commitments, except where we already possess relevant meta-commitments. Instead, it directs us away from taking on commitments of certain kinds—i.e. those we are not competent to fulfil. Since we confront inevitable uncertainty about what we will be able to do, the safest option from the point of view of trustworthiness is always to avoid commitment. But this strategy has significant costs of its own.

In chapters 5 and 6, I will discuss in more detail the extent to which any of us can individually control our commitments, or even know what these are. I will also explore the many obstacles which stand in the way of our becoming and remaining trustworthy, especially under difficult circumstances. But before moving on, I will briefly compare trustworthiness with perceived trustworthiness, and the ways in which these may make different demands upon us.

There is a difference between being trustworthy and appearing to be trustworthy. In one direction, this is obvious: con artists are adept at appearing to be trustworthy without actually being trustworthy. When we trust a con artist, we may be acting entirely reasonably, in line with the evidence we possess, but nevertheless we are making a mistake. The other direction may seem less obvious, but there are plenty of circumstances in which misleading evidence means that a trustworthy person might reasonably be regarded as untrustworthy. To invoke an epistemological cliché, I might be a paragon of trustworthiness who is constantly mistaken for my fraudster identical twin. People around me do not realize that I have a twin, and so reasonably, but inaccurately, attribute my twin's dastardly behaviour to me and thus do not trust me. More subtly, even if I lack an evil twin, people may take me to have commitments I do not really have, and thus judge me to be untrustworthy when I do not act in line with those imagined 'commitments'. We can make reasonable mistakes about one another's trustworthiness, just as we can make reasonable mistakes about kindness, diligence, courage, tastes in music, and so on.

It is tempting to regard trustworthiness as a kind of accuracy condition for trust, analogous to a truth condition for belief: beliefs can be false yet justified or true yet unjustified, and similarly trust may be inaccurate yet justified or accurate yet unjustified. But it is not evident that trustworthiness stands to trust as a constitutive aim, as many think that truth stands to belief as a constitutive aim. Trust may aim at encouraging trustworthiness, for example, rather than aiming to recognize or detect existing trust.

Even setting this complication aside, the relationship between perceived trustworthiness and trustworthiness is more complex than the relationship between, for example, perceived kindness and kindness, or perceived courage and courage. There are a number of causal and constitutive mechanisms which complicate the picture. For example, when others regard us as untrustworthy, they may give us fewer opportunities to take on commitments; this makes it more difficult for us to develop good judgement in commitment management, to learn what our capabilities are, and to demonstrate whatever trustworthiness we do have.

Even if we are able to incur commitments, lack of trust from other people can make it more difficult for us to fulfil those commitments, especially where we need cooperation and support. More generally, being trusted helps us to acquire and develop new capabilities to act—it can be difficult to learn new skills or acquire new capacities if others do not trust us to learn through trial and error, for example.

When faced with a potential new commitment, how should these complications inform our thinking? Trustworthiness, as I have argued above, by default points towards caution. If you don't take anything on, you run no risk of letting other people down. But as we can now appreciate, lack of commitment also means lack of opportunity to demonstrate our capacity to live up to a commitment, and lack of opportunity to test oneself and learn for the future. Avoiding commitment may be the best guarantee of avoiding untrustworthiness in the short term, but this is a limited strategy in the longer term even as regards trustworthiness itself, not to mention other important goals.

More generally, we should expect at least a fallible connection between being trustworthy and appearing to be trustworthy: trustworthiness could not perform its social role if it were widely undetectable. The same is true of commitments. In chapter 5, I will try to show how often our circumstances—including circumstances beyond our control—can make a difference to our ability to safely take on commitments, or to refuse commitments without penalty. To a surprising extent, our trustworthiness—or untrustworthiness—is not fully under our personal control.

Additional Sources

4.1 Trustworthiness and Commitment. On the importance of trustworthiness: (Hardin 2002; Potter 2002; Putnam 2000, 136). Potter (2002) develops a virtue account of trustworthiness, whilst McLeod (2015) outlines the range of options here. Onora O'Neill often emphasizes the importance of understanding trustworthiness, not just trust (2002a, b). Jones (2012) explores both trustworthiness and what she calls 'rich trustworthiness', which includes an ability to signal one's trustworthiness.

4.2 Trustworthiness Beyond Sincerity. This discussion connects with literature on knowledge, blame, and moral responsibility, e.g. Zimmerman (2014).

4.3 What Trustworthiness Permits. The notion of plausible deniability connects to Saul (2012)'s explorations of the distinction between outright lying and 'merely' misleading.

4.4 What Attention to Trustworthiness Can Require. Ideas around margins for error and safety draw on Williamson (2000) and the large literature inspired by Williamson's work. Our lack of a 'cognitive home' relates to work on blame, insight, norms, and excuses, e.g. Srinivasan (2015). My emphasis on the dangers of cautiously over-emphasizing trustworthiness echoes Owens (2012) on normative powers: there is value in possessing normative power, but there is also value in exercising it. The point that there is no single best way of striking a balance in this area relates to debates around 'uniqueness' in epistemology, e.g. White (2005). Hawley (2014b) connects trust and uniqueness in a somewhat different way.

4.5 Assertion and Telling. Connections to literature on epistemic injustice and silencing are taken up in later chapters, most explicitly in section 6.5. More specifically, Maitra (2010) has fruitfully explored our duties as listeners to continuing conversation, in ways which mirror some of what I say here about our responsibilities as speakers. The issues in this section can be seen through the lens of debate about norms for assertion, as I explored in chapter 3 (see references there). My somewhat different aim here is to portray the pursuit of trustworthiness as one consideration in thinking what to say, just as satisfying the epistemic-alethic norms of assertion is one consideration in thinking what to say.

4.6 Trustworthiness and Perceived Trustworthiness. Jones (2012) is very useful here, and Gambetta (2011) is a fascinating read.

5

Obstacles to Being Trustworthy

To be trustworthy, we need to avoid unfulfilled commitments. But that is easier said than done. How, in practice, can we become and remain trustworthy? The main purpose of this chapter is to show how our practical circumstances can make it more difficult for us to be trustworthy. Sometimes circumstances directly make trustworthiness harder to achieve, even when we make trustworthiness an absolute priority. Sometimes circumstances raise the cost of trustworthiness, making it more difficult to prioritize trustworthiness ahead of other goals or values. Whilst I will discuss practical action and trustworthiness in general, these points about circumstantial obstacles also apply to the special case of trustworthiness in speech, and I shall mention some issues specific to assertion along the way.

'Circumstances' here takes in our physical environment, including where we're located; our social environment, including how much support we have from others, or conversely the obstacles they may place in our paths; and our material resources, including money or lack thereof. This is not intended to be an exhaustive list. Circumstances are not just things 'outside' of us, but also include our mental and physical health or ill-health. Sometimes our circumstances are at least partially within our direct control, but sometimes they are not.

Such a wide notion may seem useless as a theoretical tool, or seem to presuppose some implausible complementary notion of the inner self, a core which remains constant across circumstances. But my main concern will be with aspects of our circumstances which are not inevitably obvious to others, or sometimes even to ourselves, and with aspects of our circumstances which may vary between different people, or for the same person over time. This combination of opacity and variation creates a number of opportunities for us to misjudge both ourselves and others, with respect to both competence and commitment, and therefore

How To Be Trustworthy. Katherine Hawley, Oxford University Press (2019). © Katherine Hawley.
DOI: 10.1093/oso/9780198843900.001.0001

with respect to trustworthiness. I will explore some of the misjudgements in chapter 6: the aim is not to provide a complete catalogue of all the ways in which we get things wrong, but to capture some key problems.

So how do our circumstances bear on our trustworthiness? In previous chapters I have developed accounts of trust, distrust, and trustworthiness which centrally involve the idea of living up to one's commitments, or, more negatively, avoiding unfulfilled commitment. Trustworthiness does not in general require us to take on specific commitments, except where these flow from earlier meta-commitments. Instead, it requires us to ensure that our commitments do not outstrip our actions. This means that in principle we have two levers at our disposal in pursuing trustworthiness: we can try to adjust our commitments, and we can try to adjust our actions. Obstacles to using these levers effectively are therefore obstacles to managing our own trustworthiness.

It is useful to distinguish two perspectives on this process of adjustment, nominally corresponding to different points in time. First, we have the opportunity to adjust our commitments—i.e. to incur or to avoid a potential new commitment. Later, we have the opportunity to act, or not, in the light of our existing commitments. From both perspectives, we need both insight and control. Someone considering whether to incur a certain commitment needs insight into what she will be able to do, insight into her competences; in addition, she needs control over whether she incurs a new commitment. If she lacks insight into her own competences, then even perfect control over her commitments will not guarantee trustworthiness, since she will not know which commitments she can safely select. If, on the other hand, she lacks control over her commitments, then even perfect insight into her own competences will not guarantee trustworthiness, since she will be unable to avoid incurring unfulfillable commitments.

The later perspective is that of someone considering action in the light of her existing commitments. This person needs insight into what her commitments (and thus trustworthiness) require of her; in addition, she needs control over her actions. If she lacks insight into her commitments, then even perfect control over her actions will not guarantee trustworthiness, since she will not know which of various incompatible actions trustworthiness requires. If, on the other hand, she lacks control over her actions for whatever reason, then even perfect insight into her commitments will not guarantee trustworthiness, since she may be unable to act as she knows her commitments require her to.

So beforehand we need insight into our competence, and control over our commitments; afterwards we need insight into our commitments, and control over our actions. This four-way distinction is much too tidy, for lots of reasons. We are constantly both facing the prospect of new commitments and trying to act in the light of existing commitments, and these tasks may interfere with one another. This interference is particularly direct when we are trying to work out whether we already have a meta-commitment which means that trustworthiness requires us to take on some new commitment. More generally, there are complex relationships between insight and control in any domain. Control is often enhanced by insight, and conversely we may gain insight into things we control, not least by experimenting through trial and error. Finally, I argued in chapter 3 that assertion involves simultaneously undertaking to speak truthfully, and speaking truthfully (or not, as the case may be): there is no time-lag involved, thus no dual temporal perspective.

Nevertheless, the four-way distinction provides a useful framework for this chapter. I aim to give some practical examples of situations which can make it difficult to be trustworthy, or force us into unappealing choices between trustworthiness and other goals, by reducing our insight or control from either the 'earlier' or the 'later' perspective. A recurring theme is the important role of our environments, material and social. Another theme is the inevitability of uncertainty, and the question of how to respond to uncertainty: possible responses to the various obstacles will be discussed in chapter 6. A third is, again, the way in which the pursuit of trustworthiness can sometimes direct us away from other important goals, values, and relationships, including sometimes the goal of communicating our own trustworthiness.

5.1 Obstacles to Controlling New Commitment

What obstacles do we encounter when trying to control what new commitments we incur? It is relatively clear how circumstances could make it more difficult for us to incur new commitments. In particular, we typically cannot commit through assertion, through promising, or through less explicit mechanisms, unless someone is willing to take us seriously. If I offer to promise, I am not bound to act unless you take me up on the offer: I need your cooperation if I am to put my trustworthiness on the line. This doesn't mean that you must believe that I will keep my promise: you might accept my promise, whilst believing that I will break it, even whilst believing that I intend to break it, indeed even whilst hoping that I will break it and thus demonstrate my untrustworthiness. Nevertheless, you need to hear and accept my offer. (I discuss related issues in chapters 2 and 3.)

Incurring commitment typically requires certain sorts of attitudes from other people. More mundanely, it often also requires the right material resources, or being in the right place at the right time. You can't take on the commitments involved in mortgage repayment unless you can first produce an initial deposit (a down payment). To take on professional commitments, you need a job, customers, or clients. More abstractly, it often takes conceptual resources and imagination to be able to make a certain commitment: someone who has never heard of Madrid cannot undertake to go there, at least not in those terms.

These are all obstacles which literally prevent people from taking on commitments; they do not merely make it inappropriate to take on a commitment because it will be too difficult to fulfil. Such obstacles have an indirect impact on how trustworthy a person can be, partly because people who lack opportunities to take on new commitments find it more difficult to develop the skills and self-knowledge required for good commitment-management. However, in terms of trustworthiness, the commitment control which matters most is not this ability to take on new commitments at will. Instead, it is our veto power, the extent to which we are able to refuse or avoid new commitments when we have doubts about whether we will be able to fulfil them. Given my account of trustworthiness in terms of avoiding unfulfilled commitments, ability to avoid commitment is crucial.

How could circumstances make this difficult? It might seem obvious that we all have the ability to refuse new commitments as we see fit, because involuntary commitment is conceptually impossible: after all, coerced promises are often regarded as non-binding, and as such not really promises at all. Maybe that's right—I won't try to argue that there can be coerced commitments, or commitments which are entirely non-voluntary, whatever that would amount to.

Even setting aside the possibility of involuntary commitment, however, there is plenty to think about in this vicinity, and plenty of opportunities for practical difficulties. First, there are certainly situations in which other people regard us as having a commitment, and yet we ourselves do not endorse that commitment. For example, suppose that I am coerced into saying 'I promise', and suppose that the coercion means that I have not genuinely made a promise. The coercion may not be visible to people around me, who therefore regard me as having freely undertaken a new commitment to act. In such situations my trustworthiness is not really at stake, given the assumption that my apparent 'promise' is not really binding. But my reputation for trustworthiness is at stake, because of other people's mistaken apprehension. We each have an interest in engaging with and trying to control other people's opinions about our commitments, and this may not be a straightforward task.

Second, practical circumstances can make it more difficult for us to be trustworthy even though our commitments are uncoerced and in a good sense still voluntary. This is because circumstances can increase the personal or social cost of refusing certain new commitments. For example, someone who has very few employment opportunities and little access to welfare benefits in some sense still has the option of turning down a demanding or degrading job, but it is much harder for her to refuse the job than it would be for someone who has other options, or an independent income. Someone working or living in a context where advancement relies upon a network of favours and reciprocity pays a high personal price if she does not take on commitments to other people when they ask her to do so, even though she could in principle decline these. More positively, it can be much harder to turn down a friend's request to commit than to turn down a stranger's request. These examples focus on practical action, but similarly our circumstances often generate various kinds of pressure or incentive to speak up rather than remain silent, and to speak assertorically rather than speculate tentatively. These pressures can be very significant, without rendering the resultant speech involuntary or coerced and thus not genuinely committing.

Different people pay different prices for refusing commitment. For example, there can be gendered differences in our expectations of who will volunteer for certain sorts of responsibilities: a woman who does not offer to bake for co-workers' birthdays (or to bring cookies to class) may be judged more harshly than a man, pressurizing her to make commitments she may find it difficult to fulfil. Small communities with high expectations of neighbourliness may disapprove of those who attempt to avoid commitment to communal activities. This sort of pressure may be invisible to outsiders: an urbanite may simply be puzzled about why the village-dweller feels pressure to undertake commitments she would prefer to avoid, and indeed may not be competent to fulfil. The varying costs of avoiding commitment can be obscure; I return to this in chapter 6 as a factor in our first-person response to such costs, and as a factor in how we evaluate others' decisions around trustworthiness and commitment.

There are many sources of pressure to take on more than just those commitments we prefer, or more than just those commitments we can easily fulfil. Such pressures are significant because they can explain why someone may become untrustworthy despite setting out with good intentions, and because some people are much more vulnerable to this pressure than are others. This isn't always a bad thing: it is a mistake to think that our lives would automatically be richer, more free, or otherwise more valuable if we were always able to pick and choose our commitments without feeling pressure from others, from their needs and desires. After all, friendship and other valuable relationships inevitably involve such constraints, and this is not a mere side effect or downside of having friends. Nor is it an unfortunate reciprocal price we must pay for being able to pressure friends to take our needs and desires into account. Instead, it is one of the ways in which friendship can shape our lives for the better. Nevertheless, depending on its sources and scale, this sort of pressure can be damaging, as I will explore in chapter 6.

Pressures to commit can arise where the person concerned knows full well what options are available to her, and what the costs and penalties of incurring or refusing commitment will be. But in practice we are often uncertain: about our options, about how our action and speech may or may not commit us, and about the consequences of all this. What does this mean for our control over commitment? It is easy to think of control and insight as closely linked, both because knowledge can be empowering, and because control facilitates learning: if I am able to adjust my behaviour and circumstances, then observe the consequences, I will better understand what commitments I have. But, as standpoint epistemologists emphasize, people who lack power may be only too aware of the nature and consequences of their own disempowerment, in ways which remain obscure to other people who occupy different, more empowered standpoints.

Indeed, Charles W. Mills (2007) has shown how those who possess power may rely upon on their own lack of insight as a means of perpetuating this possession. Mills's chief concern is with white ignorance in the context of racism, but the point generalizes. Someone employed under exploitative conditions may have an excellent understanding of how the employer's whims generate commitments for the employee, a better understanding than the employer possesses or even wants to possess; the same goes for people who are 'self-employed' in the gig economy. So for all sorts of reasons we should bear in mind that there is an important difference between having control over one's commitments and having insight into what they are; likewise, there is an important difference between lacking control over one's commitments and lacking insight into them.

Nevertheless, insight is often helpful in achieving control of our commitments. And even in relatively egalitarian company we may struggle to grasp how our speech and actions will be interpreted by others. In earlier chapters I dwelt upon explicit means of incurring commitment, through promising and assertion. But there is a host of ways in which subtle social conventions and defaults govern the incurring of less explicit commitments. In many contexts, to accept a gift, hospitality or invitation is to incur a commitment to reciprocate appropriately, whatever appropriateness turns out to require. To take a different example, often we can become committed not just by actively claiming a commitment, but also by failing to object or actively push back against others' expectations of us on this front. But it may not be clear how this opt-out works, when it is happening, and when it is already too late to protest.

It is in the nature of these conventions that they are rarely made explicit, except when we want to complain about people who violate our expectations. And they easily vary between different families, groups of friends, or workplaces, as well as across more obvious cultural divides between nations or generations. This opens up the possibility of mutual misunderstanding about what commitments different people carry, and about what it takes for those commitments to be discharged.

How does all of this confusion place obstacles in the way of our becoming trustworthy? First, suppose that you are fully aware of the social conventions governing gifts, and realize that if you accept a gift, then you will be treated as having undertaken to reciprocate with a gift at a later date: if you don't reciprocate, you will be regarded as untrustworthy. In such a situation, by accepting a gift you incur a commitment, even if you would prefer that not to be the case: we typically do not have full control over the normative significance of our actions. You can accept the gift and then say that you refuse to recognize any responsibility to reciprocate, but merely saying so does not automatically release you from commitment, any more than you are freed of promissory obligations merely by declaring that you will break an existing promise. (Things might be different if you say up-front that you will only accept the gift on condition of not being committed to reciprocate, and if the giver accepts these non-standard conditions, But such negotiations are not always binding, or even possible.)

What if you are not aware of the local convention that accepting a gift generates a commitment to reciprocate? We are often unsure of local social conventions, especially when we are outsiders for one reason or another. In such a situation, once you have accepted a gift, for example, others will think you are thereby committed to reciprocate. Is this enough to make you genuinely committed? Is your trustworthiness now on the line?

There is a theoretical dilemma here. We can insist that it is possible to incur commitment unknowingly, that sometimes we don't know that we're putting our trustworthiness on the line. Or we can insist that this is not possible, that we cannot have commitments we are unaware of. In such circumstances, other people may regard us as committed, and therefore judge our trustworthiness by our subsequent actions, but they will be mistaken. These mistakes may make it sensible for us to act as they expect, even though our trustworthiness is not genuinely on the line. But this doesn't mean that we really are committed.

Which way to jump? The dilemma invokes wider, deeper philosophical questions about norms, reasons, obligations, and first-person awareness; I am not attempting to engage those wider, deeper questions here. Instead, we can make some progress by thinking more specifically about what we need from our concepts of commitment, undertaking, trust, and trustworthiness, although this will not lead us to a precise account of exactly when commitments are incurred. In fact, I think we feel ambivalent about this in real-life situations: we feel unsure whether to judge people's trustworthiness on the basis of commitments they seem unaware of, and we feel unsure whether we must act in line with commitments others unexpectedly—mistakenly?—take us to have. This creates opportunities for guilt and for guilt-tripping, for anxiety and exploitation of different kinds.

In thinking about how far commitment can exceed the scope of first-personal grasp, we should at least agree that two extreme positions are both unappealing. It cannot be that a person is never bound by commitment unless she knows exactly what she is undertaking to do. Amongst their other roles, commitment, trust, and trustworthiness are devices for social coordination, and for reducing the so-called 'transaction costs' of trying to work together. Much of this would be impossible if lack of full transparency always voided commitments. It would also be exceptionally burdensome if we constantly had to check on each other's grasp of exactly what commitments have been incurred in order to reasonably hold people to account. Some flexibility here is a benefit to all of us, both as it enables us to trust others without detailed investigation, and as it lures us into commitments which we do not fully understand yet will ultimately value. To think otherwise is to adopt a superficially attractive but unachievable cold ideal of utterly transparent autonomy.

On the other hand, it cannot be that we have no first-person advantage whatsoever in understanding what commitments we have undertaken. Commitments can play their social role only insofar as they are available to guide our actions, at least where we are intrinsically or instrumentally motivated to be trustworthy. Indeed, we need a grasp of our existing commitments in order to judge which new commitments we can safely incur. To the extent that commitments lie beyond an individual's control or insight, they are entangled with the behaviour, attitudes, and expectations of other people. But one of the guiding themes of earlier chapters was that trustworthiness does not require us to respond to each and every demand which is placed upon us. Sometimes when people think that we are untrustworthy for not doing as they wish, those people are mistaken. Sometimes when others think we have an obligation-generating commitment to do something for them, they are mistaken. For these sorts of reasons, we need to recognize that we are not just third-party observers of our own commitments.

My remarks here blur various senses of epistemic and practical authority, without properly pinning down the relationships between these. But a concept of commitment which can underpin a useful concept of trustworthiness must picture commitments neither as wholly within the grasp of the committed person, nor as wholly beyond her. Being trustworthy is a norm, and norms often behave like this: they inhabit a space between us whereby we can each typically get some grip on how to follow the norm, but have neither a guarantee of infallibility in such matters nor complete control over whether we follow the norm. Even once we rule out the two extremes of complete first-personal veto, and assimilation of the first-personal to the third-personal perspective, there remains a lot of flexibility in how to think about commitments and trustworthiness, both as theorists and as socially embedded people.

Correspondingly our everyday practices of holding one another responsible for our apparent commitments, and thus our expectations of one another on these counts, seem somewhat shifty. Different cultural contexts, different groups of friends or workmates, can handle these issues in somewhat differing ways, allowing the individual greater or less control and insight with regard to her own commitments. This is problematic insofar as it makes life difficult for people who move between groups, and may find it difficult to work out what local practice is, or to understand their own role in local practice. These problems are most significant for people who have the most to lose from being regarded as untrustworthy; I return to these challenges in chapter 6.

Moreover social power can provide control even without insight. For example, in a high-pressure workplace, the convention could in effect be that everyone's commitments—including the boss's commitments—are whatever the boss thinks that they are. It is often an aspect of social privilege to be able to control one's commitments to a greater extent, even if we do not appreciate this. Consider the meta-commitments— commitments-to-take-on-commitments—that we often incur when entering friendships or employment. A stringent employment contract can commit you to taking on whatever commitments you are asked to take on in future; 'zero-hours' contracts make employees commit to being available at short notice, even where there is no guarantee of paid work. Some of us are more likely to suffer under such contracts than others: professional jobs typically allow much greater autonomy in choice of commitment, as compared to jobs lower down the socio-economic hierarchy. Beyond the workplace, people living in impoverished material circumstances have to impose more demanding friendships upon one another, because without social support they have no other safety net. All of these complications further illustrate that ability to control one's commitments is not uniformly or equitably distributed.

In this section I have investigated obstacles to controlling our commitments, and thus obstacles to being trustworthy. Even if we accept that there is no such thing as an involuntary commitment, practical circumstances of many kinds can make it much more difficult for people to avoid commitments, even when they are fully aware of what is going on; the price of avoiding commitment may be unaffordably high. In addition, there are many situations in which we are unsure of how our actions and speech will be understood by other people as resulting in our having incurred new commitment. Often the mere fact of others seeing us as committed gives us strong reason to act as they anticipate. But it seems that at least on occasion we do have commitments we are unaware of, generated by the social significance of our actions and words. In chapter 6 I discuss how we can or should respond to these various situations, but before doing so I will review other types of obstacle to trustworthiness.

5.2 Obstacles to Knowing One's Competence

Trustworthiness requires us to avoid unfulfilled commitments. Suppose that we have the option to incur or avoid some new commitment, that we have overcome the obstacles to control which I discussed in the previous section. What then does trustworthiness require of us? At base, the requirement is to avoid commitments that we are not competent to fulfil, given all the other demands on our time, resources, and will-power. As I discussed in chapter 4, trustworthiness does not require us to take on absolutely every commitment we can safely manage.

Trustworthiness requires us to avoid commitments we are not competent to fulfil. It does not directly impose a stricter requirement to avoid commitments unless we know that we are competent to fulfil them. Someone who blundered about at random, or took on exceptionally few commitments for selfish reasons, could through luck or parsimony reliably obey the letter of the law in terms of trustworthiness. She would incur commitments even whilst not knowing whether she was competent to fulfil them, yet luckily avoid commitments she is in fact not competent to fulfil. If she lacked insight into her own competence—and lacked insight into her own lack of competence—this would not automatically render her untrustworthy.

Nevertheless, on the assumption that we do not want to keep our commitments to the bare minimum, and do not want to rely on mere luck to render us trustworthy, we will need some insight into what we are capable of doing. So obstacles to gaining that insight are for all practical purposes obstacles to being trustworthy. Here we encounter in somewhat different guise the debates around norms for assertion and promising which I discussed in chapters 2 and 3. My strategy there was not to advocate for any particular norm, but rather to show how the existence of a range of possible norms in either case could be explained by understanding assertion as involving a promise-like commitment (and simultaneous keeping or breaking of that promise). Moreover, although norms on promise-making cannot simply be reduced to the norm of avoiding promises that will be broken, they must ultimately be understood in terms of that goal.

Given that trustworthiness prompts us to confine our commitments within the boundaries of our competence, what obstacles might get in our way? In this section, I focus on obstacles to being competent, and then on obstacles to knowing what competences we have. But first I need to clarify the conception of competence which is at stake here: what is it to be competent to fulfil a commitment? The conception which matters for trustworthiness is one which renders competence highly sensitive to the circumstances of action: what counts is successful action (including truthful speech in the context of assertion), rather than underlying skills or qualities which may be frustrated by environmental conditions before they result in successful action. This is not because successful action is all that matters in life. Nor do I imagine that success is usually possible without underlying skill or capability. It is because I have tied trustworthiness to the avoidance of unfulfilled commitment, not just to good intentions, not just to attempts to avoid unfulfilled commitment, and not just to being poised to avoid unfulfilled commitment if all goes well.

The fewer skills and capacities you have which are actionable in your environment, the fewer safe but substantive commitments you can make. Conversely, the better the match between your skills and the situations in which you act, the less often you will be forced to choose between trustworthiness and commitment, because you can have both. This is one reason why skill is valuable: it enables us to be trustworthy without sacrificing generosity, adventure, or the opportunity to learn. This is also a reason why it is valuable to live in circumstances which make it easy to act on whatever skills we possess. I will review some ways in which circumstances help determine what we can do, before discussing how circumstances also play a role in determining what we can know about what we can do.

Circumstances can be relevant to what we can do either through causal influences or more directly by constituting the circumstances under which we need to act. Causal influences here include all the very many widely recognized factors such as education, family support in childhood, physical training, inheritances, and past purchases or savings, which make each of us who we are today, with all of our skills, knowledge, material and social resources, strengths, and weaknesses.

Even granted all that history, each of us now faces different opportunities and obstacles in trying to act successfully in the world. Imagine two parents, living in different parts of the same city, both trying to get their kids to school on time every day. The first person is financially comfortable, and lives within walking distance of the school; her kids have no special medical needs or behavioural problems, and mostly enjoy school. The second person lives in cramped temporary accommodation, and can't always afford to provide breakfast; her kids have a variety of special needs, and are very reluctant to attend school. Obviously, it is easier for the first parent to get her kids to school punctually than it is for the second parent; if they switched places, as in an exploitative TV show, then their 'success rates' would change.

Let's imagine that these parents are in some intrinsic sense equally as talented and capable as each other, whatever that might mean. Nevertheless, it is much harder for one of them to act successfully in this respect than it is for the other, since they face very different challenges from the circumstances in which they must act. How should we describe this difference in terms of competence? It is politically and ethically attractive to think of both parents in my story as equally competent, noting that whilst this level of competence is sufficient for success in the easy environment, it is far from sufficient for success in the challenging environment. We might add that a parent living in difficult circumstances who does regularly get her kids to school on time thereby displays much higher levels of competence than does a parent who achieves superficially similar success whilst facing fewer obstacles.

This way of talking seems respectful of the capacities and achievements of people who must live and act in challenging environments, whether financially, socially, health-wise, or geographically. It also provides us with a way of explicating some of what is harmful about such environments: they make it much harder to turn underlying competence into concrete success. But what consequences does it have for trustworthiness and the legitimacy of taking on new commitments?

Trustworthiness requires us to be more cautious in taking on commitments where we face greater challenges to successful action. Conversely, since trust involves relying upon someone to act successfully, trust can be made appropriate or inappropriate by features of someone's circumstances, not just by her character or underlying skills: it matters where and when she is required to act. To hold all this together, I will take it that, for example, there is a competence of getting kids to school on time in an 'easy' environment, and there is a different competence of getting kids to school on time in a 'challenging' environment (in practice of course there will many more fine-grained competences even in this particular area of life). Both parents in my story have the first competence, and both lack the second one, which is much harder to develop and retain. The first parent is fortunate to live in circumstances where the first competence is all that's needed for success, and thus she can appropriately undertake to get her kids to school on time. The second parent is not, and so she risks becoming untrustworthy if she makes the analogous commitment. On this picture, a person's competences do not automatically vary with the environment, but acting in different environments requires us to use different competences, some more difficult to acquire and retain than others.

Part of what is tough about the situation of someone in difficult circumstances is precisely that she needs much more complex, high-level competences in order to succeed. This means she will more often have to choose between trustworthiness on the one hand and undertaking commitments as directed by ambition, generosity or others' demands on the other; she will more often fall into untrustworthiness even

flexible competencies

despite her best efforts. Conversely, those of us who enjoy a richly supported comfortable life should not be over-hasty to take credit for our capacity to remain trustworthy whilst simultaneously pursuing other goals and values.

So the circumstances in which we will be required to act make a difference to what competences we need to have in order to safely make a commitment without risk of becoming untrustworthy. Moreover, via different mechanisms, our past, present, and future circumstances can help or hinder us in coming to know whether we have the right competence to match a prospective commitment. I have tied trustworthiness to successful action, and thus to having the appropriate competence, and I have not tied it directly to knowing one's own competence. So in theory someone could be trustworthy without knowing what she is capable of, if through luck, isolation, or someone else's paternalistic intervention she manages to acquire only those commitments she is competent to fulfil. But, as I noted above, in practice if we are concerned to pursue trustworthiness, then knowing what we can and can't do will be crucial. What can get in the way of obtaining that knowledge?

In knowing whether we'll be able to live up to a given commitment, it helps to know the circumstances in which we will be required to act, and to know what competences we possess. There is a complex set of relationships between knowledge, uncertainty, and competence here. For example, the more competent we are, then the more confident we can be that we will live up to our commitments, whatever that turns out to mean: we can handle uncertainty about the circumstances under which we will be required to act, since our competence will serve us well across a whole range of situations. Yet if we don't know that we are highly competent, it may seem irresponsible to commit unless we are sure of what will be required of us, and sure that we can match that requirement. If we know little of what we are capable of, then knowing the circumstances in which we will need to act does not enable us to commit safely. With these interrelations in mind, I will review some obstacles to obtaining such knowledge.

The harder it is to know the circumstances under which we will be required to act, the harder it is to know whether we will succeed, to know what competence will be demanded of us in order to fulfil a given commitment. This kind of uncertainty is often generated by a combination of instability and lack of resources to compensate for unexpected setbacks. For example, suppose I wonder whether I can safely commit to giving a co-worker a lift home every evening. The more unreliable my car is, the less confident I can be; but if I have a friend who will give us both a lift on my request, or if I have enough money to pay for a taxi when my car breaks down, then I can be more confident. Suppose I wonder whether I can babysit for my sister's kids next weekend. The more unreliable my mental or physical health is, the harder it is for me to commit to babysitting.

For similar reasons, more open-ended or vague commitments are harder to incur safely, at least when we are required to surrender authority over how to make such commitments more determinate. It's easier for me to promise to come to your birthday party next weekend than it is for me to promise to come to your party whenever you decide to hold it. In general, stability or at least predictability of circumstances helps us make better judgements about likely future success. Conversely, people who have fluctuating health, who depend upon unreliable others (including unreliable authorities) for support and resources, or who deal with precarious employment or housing situations, will find it more difficult to extrapolate from their past success or failures to their ability to act successfully in the future.

Even when we know the circumstances under which we will be required to act, our past or present circumstances can make it difficult to know whether we have the competence we will need. Self-knowledge of this kind is not typically a matter of introspection. Instead, in trying to understand what actions we will successfully perform in the future, we may draw on evidence regarding the success or failure of our own past or present actions, upon evidence about the circumstances in which we have previously acted, and about our range of experience, education, and levels of motivation. There is no single recipe for coming to know what we will be able to do. Nevertheless, it is useful to pull apart different elements of the evidence available to us, and thus the different obstacles we may face in working out what commitments we will be able to meet.

Some of us have had plenty of opportunities to test our skills and learn through experience; others have had fewer. Such opportunities can help us become more competent, but the point here is that they can also help us learn what we are competent to do. Many factors are relevant: as we become older and more experienced then, so long as we are paying attention, we can learn more about our strengths and weaknesses, about what we find challenging or impossible, and about what comes easily to us. Moreover, opportunities to test our skills often require the cooperation of others: I can't practise badminton alone, or try out my latest philosophy ideas if no one will listen to me. Other times this sort of opportunity requires relatively scarce material resources, or a sufficient degree of self-confidence. Finding and exploiting such opportunities can also require us to gauge the likely consequences of failure: an important dimension of privilege is the freedom to make mistakes without being heavily penalized. It matters whether you will be given a second chance, the opportunity to change direction if early attempts at some activity are unsuccessful, or alternatively the opportunity to try again, and fail again, until you succeed.

Supposing that we have been able to act in the past, how can we judge how effective we have been? For many complex tasks, and for some less complex but intangible tasks, we lack objective measures of success or failure, or indeed a common understanding of what success amounts to. (It is no surprise that creative pursuits are especially tricky to evaluate.) Even where there is some agreement about what a successful performance looks like, we may be more concerned with relative success: in competitive situations, we don't just need to be good at performing the action in question, we need to be better than others. Sometimes the comparative judgement is easier to make than the relative judgement: perhaps I don't really know how good I am at this task, but I know at least that I'm as good as my peers. Sometimes, in contrast, we have good insight into our own capacities, whilst lacking knowledge of what others can do.

Some of us have confidence in our judgements. Some of us lack that easy confidence, but are lucky enough to be in environments where we get ready and accurate feedback on our own performances, in ways which are constructive rather than damaging. Good feedback helps us improve our future performance, but it can also give us insight into what we are doing, and the degree of success with which we are achieving it.

Lots of factors can help or hinder self-knowledge in this area, and I am not attempting to survey them all. But consideration of impostor syndrome reveals some intriguing ways in which environmental obstacles to self-knowledge can be mistakenly assimilated to mere lack of self-confidence. Impostor syndrome comes in different forms, but it can involve an inability to accept the reality of one's successes, or a tendency to attribute success to hard work, help from others, or sheer luck rather than to ability. It often also involves fear of being found out as not really deserving of accolades and opportunities one has been offered.

Trustworthiness requires us to make sensible judgements about our ability to act successfully in the future. The less well we understand our past actions, including whether and why they succeeded or failed, the harder it will be to get know what we can achieve in the future. Impostor syndrome can generate doubt about past successes, but it can also involve misunderstanding about the extent to which those successes are replicable, as opposed to mere lucky flukes. Self-regarding 'impostors' often feel that they have to make much more effort than other people. But there are many reasons why such comparative judgements may be difficult to make, especially in cultures which value effortless superiority, where trying hard is not cool.

Moreover, what we may think of as intrinsic talent or skill may be no more important to future success than are sustained effort or social support. On the one hand, skills often include the ability to adapt to changing circumstances, creatively overcoming obstacles. On the other hand, the ability to motivate oneself to great efforts is itself a transferable skill that can enable us to face new challenges. In anticipating our future success we also need to have a grasp on how far our past successes have been helped or hindered by the environments we were in. The more one identifies one's past success as a consequence of one's intrinsic abilities or skills, the more likely one is to expect future success across a range of environments. How accurate this inference is depends upon the facts of one's situation, past and future. And we don't always know how far we will control the circumstances in which we must act: supposing that our past successes have been largely due to the support of others, can we arrange for such social support in the future?

Finally, I turn to these questions of grasping our own competence as they apply to the special case of competence to speak truthfully, as required for trustworthy assertion. I have portrayed trustworthiness as a speaker as a special case of trustworthiness as a practical actor: it requires us to avoid unfulfilled commitment, which in this case means avoiding untruthful assertions. How do we judge whether we can safely commit to speaking truthfully? This requires us to assess the state of our own knowledge, to judge whether we are well-informed enough to speak up, and of course there is no general recipe for this process. Nevertheless, it is worth considering whether the challenges to assessing one's practical competence have analogues in this domain.

Is there a challenge equivalent to knowing the circumstances under which we will be required to act? Not exactly equivalent perhaps, but it is often the case that, as speakers, we are somewhat unsure what is expected of us. Is it my turn to speak? Does this person want information from me, or is she merely making small talk? Does my audience already know this fact, or is it my job to tell them? Is this a high-stakes situation in which I should be absolutely certain of what I say, or is it okay to pass along gossip or speculation?

Something like impostor syndrome can affect us as asserters, especially when we consider a slightly wider task of making a valuable, informative contribution to conversation, rather than the specific task of uttering the truth with respect to p, whatever p may be. For example, it is easy to misjudge the significance of what one has to contribute, even whilst correctly judging that the contribution would be truthful. Significance in conversation, especially group conversation, is often a relative matter, so misjudging here may also involve overestimating the significance of what others have said, or might say, and thus not realizing that it's appropriate for you to speak up rather than wait for others to contribute.

Suppose for example that women experts are less willing to pronounce about issues beyond their primary expertise than are men: Sarsons and Xu (2015) found this effect in a study of economists. Let's assume that the economists are all making good-faith efforts to be trustworthy. What then might explain these differences in willingness to take a stand? In my terms, we can understand this either as an absolute difference in economists' evaluations of how well established their own beliefs are, or else as a difference in their evaluations of how well established a belief must be in order to be made public in some context. If audiences at large respond less critically to male as opposed to female economists, then it may well be that neither group is making an error either about the grounds for their beliefs, or about the acceptability of their speaking beyond their primary expertise.

In summary, there are very many ways in which our circumstances can help or hinder us in our capacity to fulfil a given commitment, and moreover there are very many ways in which our circumstances can help or hinder our attempts to know what capacities we have. I have tied trustworthiness to the fulfilment of commitment, in other words to successful action. Obeying epistemic norms of commitment-undertaking is in that sense a derivative requirement: this is a good means of ensuring that one is trustworthy. There are many ways in which our circumstances can create obstacles both to having the competence which is required in order to fulfil a given commitment, and to knowing what competence we have.

5.3 Knowing What Commitments We Already Have

So far in this chapter I have reviewed the obstacles we face in attempting to avoid new commitments which we are not competent to fulfil. Trustworthiness also demands that we pay attention in situations where we are attempting to act in light of our existing commitments; schematically, these situations are temporally later than the ones I have been discussing so far. As I noted above, in such situations we need both insight into what our commitments require of us and the ability to align our actions (including our speech) to those requirements. In this section and the next, I look at these challenges in turn; these sections are much shorter than the ones above, since I can draw on those earlier discussions.

Often we lack insight into the significance of our speech and actions because we are unfamiliar with local conventions and expectations governing commitment. Sometimes those difficulties are resolved once we have incurred the commitment—other people's reactions may make it abundantly clear what our normative situation now is, even if that was difficult to anticipate in advance. But sometimes we just don't know what commitments we have already incurred, either because we do not know what the local conventions and defaults are or because we misremember or misunderstand our situation. Earlier, I focused on our uncertainty about how to avoid unwanted commitments, since this kind of veto power is central to trustworthiness in that context. But when taking this later perspective, we may also wonder whether we successfully managed to incur the commitments we hoped for, not just to avoid the ones we didn't want.

Incurring a commitment often requires that other people take us seriously in this regard, for example by accepting our offer to commit; taking us seriously needn't mean relying upon us to fulfil the commitment, merely regarding us as having made a commitment. But we do not always know how our words and actions have been received by others; sometimes we do not even know whether our speech has been heard, or our writing read. We sometimes come away from conversations, meetings, or email exchanges unsure of whether we managed to have our offers accepted, whether we managed to incur the commitments we hoped to incur.

Does this kind of uncertainty create an obstacle to trustworthiness? After all, trustworthiness does not require us to act only as commitment dictates: there is plenty of scope for acting beyond the scope of commitment without rendering oneself untrustworthy. So can't we accommodate this kind of uncertainty by acting as if we are committed, just to be on the safe side? I will discuss responses to uncertainty at greater length in chapter 6. But for now I note that even if we wanted to incur a commitment at some earlier time we may later prefer to be free of that commitment, perhaps because we now understand more about what it mean for us, or because a better option has come along. If we want to avoid untrustworthiness, yet prefer to act as if we are not committed, we need to know whether we really incurred a commitment earlier on, or whether we are now free to act as we choose.

This schematic temporal framing is less useful for the special case of commitment to speaking truthfully through assertion: once you know whether you have managed to make an assertion, as opposed to mere speculation, it is too late to change the content of what you say, although you might try backtracking where necessary. But it is often possible to know that you have undertaken to do or say something or other, without fully realizing the extent of what you have undertaken, and without being sure of exactly when you are being called upon to act on this commitment.

One reason for this is that our commitments are often conditional: I might have offered to help you with your project 'if I have time', or 'if you can't find anyone else', or 'if you are really stuck'. If you now call on my help, I have to judge whether those conditions are satisfied. This can involve trust in both directions. For example, you may have to trust my judgement that I genuinely don't have time; I may need to examine my own conscience on this matter. Or I may have to take your word for it that my commitment is genuinely triggered because you really are stuck, and no one else is available to help. In general, social circumstances help determine whether I can trust you when you assure me that the conditions have been satisfied, so that trustworthiness now requires me to act.

As before, in such situations we can distinguish the question of whether someone is committed to action from the question of whether other people sincerely regard her as committed to action. I have already discussed the theoretical and practical uncertainty which surrounds the role of other people's attitudes in generating commitment for us; trustworthiness is at stake only where commitment has genuinely been incurred. Depending on the framework we adopt, such uncertainties may be understood as uncertainties about what trustworthiness demands of us, or else as uncertainties about whether other people have an accurate view of what trustworthiness demands of us.

How do we know what actions are demanded by our existing commitments? Earlier, I discussed how epistemic obstacles can be generated by varying local conventions of commitment. Such obstacles are also relevant to this later temporal perspective, when we are trying to establish what commitments we have already incurred. In particular, cultural dislocation can make it more difficult to know whether our offers to commit have been taken seriously: if I suggest a lunch meeting, and you don't demur, have you thereby accepted my offer to commit to showing up, or have you merely evaded the issue? These interactions can be a little confusing at the best of times, but we are all the more prone to misunderstandings when we are new to a country, a workplace, or a social circle.

As I will discuss in chapter 6, the flexibility with which we can choose to respond to such uncertainties may depend a great deal upon our social power, our ability to access alternative options, and the importance to us of maintaining a reputation for trustworthiness. Some of us, some of the time, can get away with simply blundering on through our hazy grasp of existing commitments; some of us certainly cannot.

5.4 Controlling Our Actions

Finally, following my four-way taxonomy of obstacles to trustworthiness, I should consider obstacles to acting in line with our commitments, even once we know what our existing commitments are. This may be the broadest category of obstacles—obstacles to action in general. As such, it does not require special efforts to demonstrate that challenging circumstances can generate difficulties on this front: it is obvious that our circumstances affect how we can act. By definition, challenging circumstances make it more difficult to act as we would like to do.

Correspondingly, this is the category where I have found least scope for saying something which is distinctively relevant to trustworthiness. This may be because it follows the preceding three sections: if we could successfully overcome obstacles in all of the other three categories, then there would be no special problem here. Obstacles to action are obstacles to trustworthiness only when we have acquired a commitment which demands that action of us. But if we already knew that a given commitment would require us to act in a way which we would find difficult, and if we had the freedom to decline that commitment without much cost, then we could simply avoid getting into a situation where that obstacle to action made it harder for us to be trustworthy. This might be a matter of great regret, of course, if we have other reasons to want to act in that way, with or without a commitment to doing so. But in itself it would not diminish our trustworthiness.

Are there obstacles to appropriate action in the special case of assertion—i.e. fulfilment of commitment to speak truthfully regarding the matter at hand? Of course it is often not easy to have the knowledge required for appropriate assertion. This is not a direct obstacle to trustworthiness: one can be trustworthy without having much knowledge or competence, provided one can avoid becoming overcommitted. But as we will see in the following chapter, lack of competence, and thus an increased requirement to choose between trustworthiness and new commitment, brings troubles of its own.

More direct challenges are faced by those who must communicate in languages they have not mastered, those with speech or literacy difficulties, or those who face other practical challenges to self-expression. Treating assertion as simultaneous incurring and discharging (or not) or commitment generates some complications here. For more ordinary commitments to future action, there is a clear difference between controlling what I am committed to doing (as discussed in section 5.1) and controlling what I in fact do (the topic of this section). But with assertion, control and lack of control over various different matters is entangled.

I need control over whether I am making an assertion, as opposed to remaining silent or else performing some other speech act. I need control over the content of what I say, in the sense of controlling whether I am making an assertion as to whether p or an assertion as to whether q. Finally, I need control over whether or not I speak truthfully, whether I get it right as between saying that p and saying that not-p. These different demands are obscured by the more standard philosophical habit of discussing assertion that p as opposed to assertion as to whether p. But it is important to see that I may have more or less control on each of these various fronts. Thus anything which limits my control in one of these respects may make it more difficult for me to be trustworthy.

I began this chapter by setting up a four-way taxonomy: before versus after, commitment versus competent action. I conceded immediately that in thinking about obstacles to control and insight on these various fronts, it's often not easy to fit challenges into just one quadrant of that four-way taxonomy. Nevertheless, it should now be clear that there are many ways in which our circumstances of all kinds can generate obstacles to our pursuit of trustworthiness; correspondingly, that circumstances can also make it easier for us to pursue trustworthiness. These challenges and choices may or may not be apparent to us in the first person, and they may or may not be apparent to interested onlookers who are tempted to make judgements about our trustworthiness, and even about our character.

In the next chapter, I will examine the dilemmas and double binds which can confront us in responding to the inevitable obstacles we face to pursuing trustworthiness, especially when others are likely to misunderstand the constraints we are working within.

Additional Sources

5.1 Obstacles to Controlling New Commitment. Relevant literature includes debates around coerced promises, and the nature of promises more generally: see sources listed in chapter 2, and in particular Shiffrin (2014). Hawley (2018a) discusses coerced speech. There are also connections between the themes of this section and debates around illocutionary force and silencing, e.g. Langton (1992), Hornsby and Langton (1998).

Kukla (2014) is also important here, and I discuss connections with Kukla's paper more explicitly in section 6.5. Peet (2015) explores other respects in which it may be difficult to control what we commit to through speech. See also Bird (2002), Dougherty (2015), and E.Fricker (2012). The issues discussed in this section around control bear some relation to feminist theorizing about autonomy, as reviewed by Stoljar (2013).

5.2 Obstacles to Knowing One's Competence. The relationship between competence and circumstances outlined here owes something to Hawley (2003). More broadly, the vexed question of how competence relates to success echoes debates about virtue, dispositions, reliabilism, and generics elsewhere in philosophy. Sakulku and Alexander (2011) is a useful overview of psychological research on impostor syndrome, and I explore these issues at greater length in Hawley (2019). Intemann (2010) provides a good entry point into feminist standpoint epistemology.

5.3 Knowing What Commitments We Already Have. Sources listed under 5.1 are relevant here.

5.4 Controlling Our Actions. Just as this is the section where there seems least scope for raising issues distinctive to trustworthiness, it is also the section where it seems least feasible to pick out individual sources for the idea that we cannot always act as we would like.

6

Consequences

In chapter 5, I explored a variety of ways in which our circumstances can make it more difficult for us to avoid unfulfilled commitment, and thus more difficult for us to be trustworthy. I discussed in turn (i) obstacles to controlling commitment (some but not all of which arise from epistemic obstacles); (ii) obstacles to knowing our competences; (iii) obstacles to knowing what commitments we have already incurred; (iv) obstacles to acting as commitment requires us to do. There is no sensible way of generalizing about these obstacles, except to note that they often arise from our social and material situations, not just our internal or mental states, and that they are not always clearly visible either to ourselves or to others. Many of these obstacles can be understood not as making trustworthiness impossible, but instead as raising the cost of trustworthiness, either by making it harder to avoid unfulfillable new commitments or by making it harder to act in line with existing commitments.

Given that all of us face these obstacles to some degree or other, how should we respond if we care about trustworthiness? In reacting to or anticipating these obstacles, we often face uncomfortable choices between prioritizing trustworthiness and prioritizing other important goals and values. For example, from the narrow perspective of preserving trustworthiness, it is usually safer to avoid commitment wherever possible. But followed to the letter this is a recipe for a lonely, unrewarding life, one which benefits neither the recipe-follower nor the people around her. I touched upon this sort of dilemma in chapter 4, and will explore a range of similar issues in this chapter: the pursuit of trustworthiness can come into conflict with any number of other goals.

I have found no completely systematic way of reviewing the ways in which we may respond to challenges, nor the kinds of goals or values which may conflict with the pursuit of trustworthiness. So instead of

How To Be Trustworthy. Katherine Hawley, Oxford University Press (2019). © Katherine Hawley.
DOI: 10.1093/oso/9780198843900.001.0001

trying to discuss every possibility, I will focus on interactions between our responses to such challenges on the one hand, and other people's interpretations or misinterpretations of our speech and actions on the other. These interactions take several forms. For example, the way in which we respond to obstacles may be guided by our expectations of what others already think of us, or what they will think of us if we take a certain action. Indeed, some of the obstacles are generated by our need to take other people's opinions into account, and by our difficulties in doing so. Moreover, our reactions to certain obstacles raise the chances of our being misinterpreted by other people. This is especially likely when our circumstances, or the ways in which our circumstances make trustworthiness more difficult, are not transparent to the people around us.

6.1 How We See Each Other

Much of my discussion is framed from the perspective of someone who is struggling to be trustworthy whilst pursuing other important goals and values, someone who is evaluated by other people around her. But I also need to consider the perspective of those other people, for two reasons. First, of course, each of us is also 'other people'. That is, we make judgements and interpretations of people's words and actions, in the light of what those words and actions suggest about commitment, competence, and trustworthiness. It's crucial that we do this well, since poor judgement in this area can be damaging both for the person who makes a mistake, and for the person who is on the receiving end of the misjudgement or misinterpretation. This book focuses on how to be trustworthy, but it is also important that we understand how to evaluate other people's trustworthiness.

Second, when we are thinking about how to act, about how to balance the pursuit of trustworthiness with other goals, in light of whatever obstacles we encounter, then we often need to anticipate and accommodate other people's opinions of us. Sometimes the most trustworthy course of action is not the course of action which will appear most trustworthy to those around us, and in such situations we face some tricky decisions.

My account of trustworthiness in terms of avoiding unfulfilled commitment provides a distinctive framework for understanding these issues, though as ever it does not provide neat and tidy resolutions. Commitment and competence are logically separate: one can behave competently whilst free of commitment, and of course one can have commitments one is not competent to fulfil, even though that makes for untrustworthiness. In chapter 5 I treated commitment and competence (as linked to successful action) as independent levers which we control imperfectly, trying to bring our commitments in line with our competence to act, and our actions in line with our existing commitments.

But from the observer's perspective, there are inferential links around the triad of trustworthiness, competence, and commitment, links which rely upon the conceptual connections between these. Perhaps most obviously, we can base judgements about other people's trustworthiness on our judgements (or misjudgements) of their competence and commitments. If you regard someone as having undertaken a commitment, yet fail to recognize that her actions are in line with that commitment, then you will mistakenly infer that she is untrustworthy. Someone who finds it difficult to get others to recognize her successful actions therefore has an incentive not to take on such commitments in the first place. Otherwise she risks being unfairly regarded as untrustworthy.

Conversely, if you mistakenly think that someone has undertaken a commitment, and accurately recognize that her actions are not line with that purported commitment, then you will mistakenly infer that she is untrustworthy. Someone who is often misunderstood in this way therefore has an incentive to behave as other people think that she should, even if her commitments do not really require her to act in that way. In the special case of speech, this is the situation of someone who is inadvertently taken to be making assertions when she intends only to speculate or question, and so must be cautious about what she says.

But these inferences can also run from trustworthiness to competence or commitment. If you regard someone as trustworthy, then you can draw conclusions about her competence from what you take her commitments to be, and vice versa. After all, a trustworthy person will avoid commitments which are unmatched by competence. For example if your friend offers to drive you to the station, and you regard her as trustworthy, then you simply assume that she has access to a car and knows how to drive: she would not have offered otherwise. You infer from commitment and trustworthiness to competence.

To take another example, suppose that you are chatting with your wheelchair-using friend, someone you regard as trustworthy. You talk about your plans for a group hike and picnic, and your friend says 'that sounds great, I'd love to come along'. If you assume that your friend's wheelchair means that she can't participate in a hike, you may assume that she is politely or wistfully endorsing your plans, which don't include her. You infer from trustworthiness and lack of competence to lack of commitment; after all, she would not undertake to do something she cannot manage. If instead you are open to the idea that your friend is competent to participate in a hike (if you choose an accessible route), then you can hear your friend's words as a commitment to come along, indeed as an expression of her trust in you to make this feasible. Dropping the assumption that she lacks competence on this front blocks the inference to a lack of commitment.

When we take people to be trustworthy, and regard them as lacking competence in some respect, we can infer that they do not have a commitment which requires that competence. Moreover we can also infer that they would not take on such a commitment even if we invited them to do so. After all, trustworthiness involves an effort to avoid commitments unmatched by competence. Such inferences colour our interpretation of what others say, as in the case of the (in)accessible hike. But they also affect the way in which we think prospectively about issuing invitations or offers, and about asking for help or expertise. There is no point asking a trustworthy yet incompetent person, since she will have to decline any potential commitment. Mistakes and misjudgements on this front seem compatible with at least superficial well-meaningness, and a positive outlook on the other person's moral character: it's exactly because we admire the other person's trustworthiness that we infer from our low opinion of her competence to a low expectation of her commitments.

As a special case of this inferential pattern, when we take a speaker to be trustworthy we may use the content of what she says as a guide to the force with which it is being expressed. For example if someone says something which appears ludicrously implausible, we may infer that she is joking, or being sarcastic, or speaking metaphorically. Such an inference seems to depend upon an assumption about what the speaker is likely to know: she must know how implausible this claim is, and she's a sensible (trustworthy) person, so surely she can't seriously be asserting it? Likewise, it is disconcerting when someone appears to be asking a question to which we believe she already knows the answer: in such situations, we cast about for alternative explanations, perhaps wondering whether the speaker is in fact asserting the proposition via a merely rhetorical question. In such cases, we're making a judgement about competence and then basing a judgement about commitment upon it, again mediated by a positive view of the speaker's trustworthiness.

So when we take somebody to be trustworthy we use this premise to make inferences between her competence (or lack of competence) and commitment (or lack of commitment). This is one reason why it is useful for us to have well-grounded views about others' trustworthiness. It also highlights a mechanism via which misjudgements on any of these three points—trustworthiness, competence, commitment—can ramify.

Imagine a senior professional who manages and is supported by an administrator. The administrator's explicit job description includes duties such as handling appointments, drafting documents, and keeping track of information. Making coffee for the manager is not part of the job description, yet the manager expects the administrator to make coffee, and is disposed to regard her as violating a job-related commitment if she does not.

If the administrator doesn't make coffee, she regards herself as meeting all her commitments, but the manager will regard her as not fully trustworthy. If the administrator tries to bypass the issue, for example nudging someone else into making the coffee, she risks looking even more untrustworthy in the manager's eyes. But if she conforms to expectations and makes coffee, this can create other problems. First, it may in time generate a real commitment: ongoing silent conformity to unreasonable expectations can make them reasonable. Second, she does not get credit for going beyond the call of duty to be generous or hospitable, only for doing what her job requires. In these ways the administrator is worse off than someone who 'volunteers' to make coffee. Third, the administrator has less time to fulfil her other commitments at work, which has potential consequences for her trustworthiness.

We can multiply the complications. Suppose that administrators often end up making coffee for male managers and not female ones, either because the different managers have different expectations or because the expectations of female managers carry less weight. Then female managers either have to insist on the coffee, conforming to a 'bitch' stereotype, or else lose face by making their own coffee. In a workplace where 'real' bosses have someone to make coffee for them, this has further negative consequences.

There are multiple layers of error and misjudgement available to everyone involved in such situations. Most obviously, it can be difficult for someone entering a new context to appreciate what the local conventions and practices are, and so to appreciate what commitments she may be taken to have incurred by certain actions—this is an obstacle that I discussed in chapter 5. But in addition, such difficulties can themselves be obscure: people already embedded in their practices often underestimate how hard it can be for newcomers to get a grip on what's going on. Then old hands may tend to see unfulfilled commitment as a consequence of intentional neglect or carelessness, rather than as a consequence of an easy misunderstanding. Finally, the fact that expectations may be informal or implicit makes it more difficult to challenge them without seeming picky or unreasonable.

Again, I am not attempting to impose rigorous order onto all the many expectations, inferences, judgements, and misjudgements we encounter in our various social roles. But it should be clear that our beliefs and assumptions about other people's competence, commitments, and trustworthiness are mutually reinforcing. When someone says or does something we find surprising, we often have a choice about how to adjust our beliefs. If someone expresses a claim we find initially implausible, do we take it more seriously because of our respect for the person saying it, or do we take this implausibility to suggest either that the speaker is not really being serious or else that she is less knowledgeable than we had imagined? Similarly, when someone acts in a way which we find surprising given our assumptions about her commitments and trustworthiness, we again have a choice about how to adjust our beliefs. Taking care over such choices, assumptions, and inferences is an important element of trying to treat other people fairly.

Shifting back to our perspective as agents trying to decide how to act, speak, and incur commitment: we must take into account the ways in which others are likely to judge or misjudge us, especially when we are faced with various obstacles to being trustworthy. There are self-interested reasons for being able to communicate one's trustworthiness, but this is also a service to others, especially when we're trying to be trustworthy as sources of information in particular. When we fulfil our practical commitments to other people, they can benefit even before they know that we have fulfilled those commitments. If I keep my promise to take care of your garden whilst you're away, then I help you even before you know that I have done so. In contrast, if I commit to speaking truthfully, and I do speak truthfully, my audience cannot profit from this if they do not trust me. The social value of trustworthiness in speech is tied very closely to its being recognized as such.

6.2 Responding to Limited Control of Our Commitments

Although trustworthiness requires us to avoid unfulfilled commitments, it is not always straightforward for us to avoid tricky commitments in the first place, as I explored in section 5.1. Often we do not fully understand the significance of our speech or actions, so we blunder into incurring new commitments. And it is sometimes difficult to avoid commitment even when we know exactly what is going on. For example, when we have already incurred a meta-commitment—a commitment to take on certain types of new commitment as they arise—then trustworthiness requires us to follow through even when we have doubts about our ability to fulfil the proposed new commitment. In other situations, pressure to take on new commitments can arise from a lack of attractive alternatives.

Suppose then that we encounter circumstances in which we find it difficult or costly to avoid incurring a new commitment, whether we like it or not, and whether or not we feel competent to fulfil that commitment. How to respond? We could choose to bite the bullet, and pay the high price of prioritizing trustworthiness by avoiding new commitment. For the most part, the cases I discussed in chapter 5 do not involve a complete lack of control over commitment, and indeed there is reason to think that coerced commitments do not genuinely bind us. Instead, I focused on situations in which our circumstances mean that avoiding commitment is a very unattractive option.

For example, someone who has only one friend, a person who makes unreasonable demands upon her, may be forced to choose between accepting unsafe commitments (thus risking untrustworthiness) and losing her only social contact. Someone who needs to see a doctor, and will struggle to make it to the appointment on time because she relies upon poor public transport, must choose between a risky commitment to show up on time and a certainty of not seeing the doctor at all. People living in challenging circumstances, with few material or social resources, will more often pay a very high price if they prioritize trustworthiness—the avoidance of unfulfilled commitment—over other needs or desires. Some such costs must be imposed on others: imagine that it is a child who needs medical attention, but the parent who must undertake to get them to the doctor's. It is broadly possible to decide not to make a commitment in such circumstances, but the practical, personal, and social cost is high.

In other situations, we cannot simply decide not to accept commitment, even if we are willing to pay the price of this choice. Whether or not we incur a new commitment is often not a matter of direct choice. For example, when we are unclear about how our actions or speech may commit us, it is hard to know how to implement a decision not to take on a new commitment. Both the demanding friend and the distant doctor cases can be understood as epistemically transparent to the person concerned: she knows what it would take to incur, or not to incur, this commitment, and she understands the costs and risks associated with each option. But in other situations we have difficulties in understanding what sorts of words or actions will land us with new commitments, ones we may be reluctant or unwilling to fulfil.

How can we handle such situations? One strategy is to try to create a margin of safety, to avoid doing anything with even a hint of possible commitment attached. In practical terms this would mean not accepting any kind of favours, not doing anything which might call for reciprocation, not showing interest in possible commitments, and so on. For the special case of potentially informative speech, this strategy might appeal to someone who struggles to control the force of her speech, and cannot reliably prevent it from becoming an assertion: she might try to speak as little as possible since she cannot be sure of making her speech suitably tentative. (The opposite problem—difficulty in getting taken seriously—is also significant, but not such a direct obstacle to trustworthiness.) People in such situations pay a double price: they avoid the commitment they are concerned to avoid, but as collateral damage they also avoid commitments they would happily incur, if they could be safely chosen without thereby also incurring unsafe commitments.

A related strategy is to try to take back control by making exaggeratedly explicit efforts to communicate about what commitments one is willing to incur. Often we are liable to incur commitments by failing to push back against others' expectations, or by failing to explicitly specify which commitments we reject. We can't always tell exactly when and where such defaults and implicit expectations apply, so this strategy recommends being as explicit as possible wherever there is potential doubt.

For example, suppose you have an idea or information which you would like to raise for consideration, but without giving your full assurance of its truth. The safest option, short of remaining silent, is to say explicitly that this is just a guess, that you shouldn't be relied upon, that you're just suggesting or speculating, and so on. Or suppose that you would like to accept an invitation to dinner, but do not want to commit to reciprocating. You can try saying that you would love to come to dinner but you won't be able to return the favour. Or suppose that you would like to have an appointment kept open for you at the doctor's office, yet don't want to commit to showing up on time. You could try saying just that. In general, you might do something whilst disavowing its standard social significance, or else conditionally offer to do something so long as it does not involve you in unwanted commitment. Under the right circumstances, this can be a smart strategy for pursuing trustworthiness: it puts the ball in the other person's court, and, if successful, allows us to regain control over the incurring of commitment.

As ever, there are complications. Such moves often invoke some kind of excuse for not incurring the commitment in question. Lack of competence here seems a better excuse than lack of willingness, at least amongst friends. For example, if you are trying to accept a dinner invitation without undertaking to reciprocate, then it is acceptable to cite your health problems, your over-crowded house share, or your limited cooking skills. It is not so nice to say simply that you don't like entertaining, or can't be bothered to cook—it takes nerve to request commitment-free dinner on those grounds.

But we may struggle to know which excuses for avoiding commitment will be accepted without social cost, and which will not, leaving us with the commitment plus the negative consequences of having tried to avoid it. A hard-pressed doctor's receptionist, for example, is unlikely to give us permission to just try to show up, especially if appointments are over-subscribed. If there is a formal or informal penalty for missing appointments, we can't easily ask to be excused, no matter how tough our circumstances, and asking for special consideration may itself attract censure. Similarly, it's not always possible to avoid the perceived commitments associated with assertion even when we include hedging terms—under such circumstances the safer option is not to speak at all.

How might all of this manoeuvring look to observers who are not fully aware of the challenges posed by circumstances? From this outside perspective, imagine someone who opts to pay the high social cost of avoiding a particular commitment. Suppose we do not realize how difficult it will be for that person to fulfil that commitment, or at least how difficult it is for her to know what she can do; perhaps it's the kind of thing that would be easy for us to manage. Then the refusal to become committed looks perversely unmotivated: we may simply assume that she is antisocial, lacking confidence, or not a 'team player'.

Or imagine someone who makes what seem to be absurdly cautious attempts to specify exactly what she can and can't commit to doing, offering up conditions and potential excuses. Again, imagine that we do not appreciate how difficult it is for this person to know whether she will be able to act as required, perhaps because she knows how unstable or hostile her circumstances are likely to be. To us, the person will appear to be simply a fusspot, or self-centred, or unreliable: we won't see these superficially irritating behaviours as evidence of her admirable underlying motive.

I argued in chapter 5 that people are more likely to face obstacles to controlling their commitments if they are living in difficult circumstances—different types of difficulty generate different types of obstacle. My point in the present section is that such difficulties can be compounded by attempts to compensate for or overcome these obstacles: all the more so when someone is struggling to control her commitments, and struggling to compensate for this, all whilst dependent on the opinions of people around her who do not appreciate the dilemmas and challenges she is grappling with. The pursuit of trustworthiness requires greater sacrifices from some people than from others, and, what is worse, those sacrifices may be mistaken for fussiness or flakiness.

So far in this section, I have pictured cases in which a relatively powerless person tries to protect herself both from becoming untrustworthy and from paying other costs, and cannot achieve these simultaneously. But there are parallel issues which affect relatively powerful people, and not always to their advantage. Sometimes an individual has special responsibility to foresee and either forestall or accommodate possible misapprehensions of the intended force of her words. For example, distinctions between informing, warning, and threatening may be very subtle. Suppose that an employer faced with workers striking to retain their pensions says to them that if the strike succeeds then other important benefits will be lost, in order to balance the books financially. This could be understood as providing a piece of information, or as a helpful warning, or as a sinister threat; let us suppose it is intended merely to be informative. Given the power of the employer, and the heightened atmosphere of a strike, it is not enough for the speaker to take ordinary measures to communicate her intention merely to inform; she has a responsibility to exercise extraordinary care in this matter, perhaps even to recognize that in such circumstances there is no possibility for her merely to inform without threatening, or at least without being widely understood as threatening. Not every speech act is available under every circumstance.

There are many other situations—for example, as an expert witness in the courtroom, or when electioneering—in which the speaker's responsibility is not limited to incurring only those commitments she is competent to fulfil. In such situations speakers also have responsibilities to communicate clearly, to avoid misunderstandings and unwanted implicatures in terms of both force and content, to ensure that others have an accurate grasp of what commitments she has incurred. Sometimes in such heightened circumstances there is no way for a speaker to ask an 'innocent question' or merely to speculate; one form of disingenuousness is to insist on the non-committal nature of one's words when one knows how easily they can be misconstrued.

6.3 Responding to Obstacles to Grasping Our Competence

When we are struggling to avoid new commitments we are not competent to fulfil, we can focus on avoiding commitments, as I explored in the previous section. Alternatively or additionally, we can try to become more competent, or at least become more knowledgeable about our strengths and weaknesses. We can try to become more competent by developing skills, knowledge, and resources. But recall that I have pinned competence to the circumstances of action: to fulfil a certain commitment, one needs to be competent to act successfully wherever, whenever, and however that commitment calls for action. So another way of attempting to improve one's competence is by adjusting the circumstances in which one will need to act, in the hope of creating a situation in which one is capable of acting successfully.

This will mean different things for different people, depending on the resources they have available and the types of unwanted or uncertain commitment they are liable to incur. But it will often mean avoiding risks, avoiding situations which overstretch one's capabilities, and trying to stay close to existing networks of support. This can feel like a positive integration into the community. But it is also a way in which perceived lack of control over one's commitments, together with a potential high penalty for untrustworthiness, push us to stay close to home, both literally and metaphorically.

Managing the circumstances in which you will need to act can sometimes mean managing other commitments. For example, suppose that you know how difficult it is for you to avoid unwanted commitments, yet you want to retain the capacity to fulfil such commitments if you do end up landed with them. One strategy is to decline as many commitments as you can, even commitments which you would value, and which you could comfortably fulfil so long as nothing else came up. That way you keep yourself relatively flexible, in order to try to cope with those commitments you cannot avoid. For example, if you have a demanding boss, and know you will be unable to turn down 'requests' for late working, then you may choose not to make social arrangements with friends and family, so that you don't end up having to let them down when new work commitments are imposed upon you. This sort of behaviour may seem especially puzzling to onlookers who don't realize your vulnerability to your boss: your efforts to remain trustworthy look like a self-centred unwillingness to socialize.

Looking beyond the strategy of becoming more competent, what about trying to become more knowledgeable of one's existing competence? We can try to reduce the relevant uncertainties. For example, we may pursue cautious enquiry, attempting to make things more explicit, investigating and questioning before we take on new commitments; such investigation may be directed towards the expectations of the person asking us to take on a commitment, towards the circumstances in which we will need to act, or towards our own strengths and weaknesses. The more successful we are in such enquiries, the more we will understand what we may be undertaking to do, and the more we will understand our chances of being able to fulfil such a commitment.

This kind of caution is not cost-free. In itself it uses up time, energy, and other resources; by assumption this challenge often affects people who don't have a lot of time, energy, or resources to spare. But in addition such caution can either improve or damage our image in the eyes of people around us. Careful examination and weighing of potential commitments may be seen—often rightly—as a sign of trustworthiness, of being the kind of person who takes commitments seriously and is anxious not to incur debts that cannot be repaid. On the other hand, if this is read as ostentatious or excessive caution it can prompt impatience in those around us, who wish we'd just make up our minds.

To some extent, different reactions to such caution may be linked to disagreements about what I earlier called 'meta-commitments'. In the context of an ongoing relationship, whether professional or personal, one person may view another as having already committed to taking on new commitments, to accepting new requests or tasks, for example. If that's the expectation, then overscrupulousness about new commitments can itself be seen as a form of untrustworthiness, a violation of previous commitment.

In our wider lives, we can afford to take different attitudes to different people: you'd like an accountant, an electrician, or a car mechanic to be cautious, whilst that's not necessarily what you want from the assistant at the local shop, the restaurant waiter, or indeed your friends. Different people may want different things from their doctors, whether that be caution or quick reassurance; likewise we are sometimes conflicted about what we want from the politicians who are supposed to represent us.

A different tactic for trying to reduce uncertainty about future capacity to act involves attempting to stabilize one's circumstances. Stable circumstances do not necessarily make it easier to act, but they at least make us more knowledgeable about whether we will be able to act. There are situations in which we might be forced to choose just one of these. That is, we may need to choose between stabilizing a situation in such a way that it makes it foreseeably difficult for us to act, or instead allowing less stability but with the possibility of easier action. This is yet another way in which the pursuit of trustworthiness can conflict with other goals. Stable situations make it easier for us to be trustworthy (we can know what we will and won't be able to do), but unstable situations leave open at least the possibility that we will be able to act as we would like to do.

In many ways, the discussion here echoes my discussion in earlier sections of this chapter. Our responses to lack of control over commitments and our responses to lack of insight into our competence overlap and interact. This is because in both cases the most cautious response is to try to avoid becoming committed in the first place. Where we act cautiously in regard of commitment, either because we know we will find it difficult to fulfil a commitment or because we are unclear what we will manage, then we pay a price both in terms of sacrificing our own personal goals and in terms of our public reputation.

How might any of these strategies be misinterpreted? Where others do not realize that we lack competence for certain tasks—perhaps because they don't realize how few resources we have, how many other demands we encounter, or the precariousness of our health—they may fail to understand why we are turning down commitments we could fulfil, or why we are being so cautious about throwing ourselves into new circumstances of action. Moreover, if others don't realize how difficult it is for us to know what we are capable of—for example because they don't know what evidence is available to us, or because they don't appreciate our lack of self-confidence—then they may struggle to understand other aspects of our behaviour.

We use these strategies in an attempt to preserve our trustworthiness, and our reputation for trustworthiness. But they are easily misunderstood by people who think we could preserve our trustworthiness without taking these measures; such misunderstanding can lead them to reach for other, less flattering explanations of our behaviour.

6.4 Retrospective Perspectives

I turn now to situations in which we are trying to act in the light of whatever existing commitments we have. In chapter 5 I briefly discussed difficulties in knowing what commitments we already have, and difficulties in acting appropriately. How can we respond when we are unclear about what commitments we have already incurred? In a narrow sense, it is always safer to bring my actions in line with a 'commitment' I think I might have incurred. After all, trustworthiness does not require us to avoid actions we have not undertaken to do: we are free to act beyond our commitments. But there is always a risk of becoming untrustworthy by failing to do something I have in fact committed to doing.

This strategy of trying to accommodate all epistemically possible commitments cannot be turned into a viable general policy, for two types of reason. First, my various for-all-I-know commitments may demand conflicting actions, and so there may be no way of living up to all of these 'commitments'. These sorts of conflicts can arise even with genuine commitments, even for people who are scrupulously careful about what they take on: it is not always feasible to predict whether different commitments will make incompatible demands upon us. But the more difficult it is to know whether one has a commitment, the more likely that it is impossible to accommodate all epistemically possible commitments.

Second, trying to live by my for-all-I-know commitments even where these do not conflict will make it difficult for me to pursue other goals and values, including personal relationships, and to follow other-oriented impulses to generosity, or spontaneity. Imagine what it would be like to live this way: like having a manipulative boss or emotionally abusive partner, someone who imposes upon you by leaving you uncertain what you are supposed to do, yet sure of being penalized if you don't do the 'right' thing. We cannot be required to impose this kind of stress upon ourselves.

None of us can avoid all risk of becoming somewhat untrustworthy, because we all have some uncertainty about what we have committed to doing, and it is not feasible to accommodate this uncertainty by doing things 'just in case'. However the severity of this risk depends upon several factors. It matters how many obstacles there are to knowing our commitments, for example how difficult it is for us to understand our local social environment. It matters what penalties there are for having unfulfilled commitment. And it matters what skills, time, and resources we have available to try to act 'just in case'.

How does this look to other people? If it seems clear to other people that we know what our commitments are, then of course they will regard us as knowingly violating trust when we do not act in line with those commitments. And there are lots of reasons why other people's ignorance of our circumstances, and of the significance of our circumstances, makes it hard for them to appreciate that we may not know what our commitments are. For example, people who have never lived outside of their original class background, or national culture, or local neighbourhood, may underestimate how hard it is for other people to acclimatise when entering that situation. It is easy to underestimate the ways in which newcomers may be mystified about what is expected.

If we find it difficult to know what commitments other people will take us to have, then we need to be extra cautious if we want to develop a reputation for trustworthiness. But other people may not realize that this is the reason for our caution, generating resentments of different kinds. Such misunderstandings are more likely to occur when people from different cultures or backgrounds meet. Controversial empirical studies of levels of 'generalized trust' in multicultural neighbourhoods have suggested that trust levels in such areas are low. One potential explanation of this finding is that levels of generalized trust are lower in lower-income areas; the less you have, the less you can afford to take risks in trusting other people, and when you know that other people have little, you may well think that they cannot afford to be trustworthy at their own expense. However a complementary factor may be mutual misunderstandings, or differences of opinion, about what actions and behaviours trustworthiness requires. This may be as mundane as expectations about what to do with household rubbish, noise levels at different times of the day, or responsibilities to children out playing in the street.

I argued in section 6.1 that conceptual connections between trustworthiness, commitment, and competence support inferences between these three. Sympathetic observers who mistakenly think that we know what our commitments are may assume that we are incompetent if we do not act as those supposed commitments require. After all, the alternative is for them to regard us as intentionally violating trust. This is true when others don't appreciate our difficulties in understanding what commitments we have, and it is also true when others don't realize how hard it is for us to act in the circumstances in which we find ourselves.

6.5 Testimony and Testimonials

Throughout this book I have treated speech as a special case of action: being trustworthy as an informant is a special case of being trustworthy as a practical agent. This builds upon a picture of assertion as involving commitment to speak truthfully (chapter 3). I have drawn on examples from speech as well as other types of action in discussing the demands which trustworthiness places upon us, the practical obstacles we encounter, and the tricky choices we must sometimes make in the face of those obstacles. In my view, this integrated treatment helps us towards a better understanding of a range of philosophical issues arising both from testimony and from other practical actions, whether or not the reader agrees with me on the details of that understanding.

How does this project relate to philosophical work which is focused more narrowly on testimony? I see my work as complementing and extending that literature, rather than attempting to replace or undermine it, since there are some significant issues which I have not tried to address. In particular, I have neglected a key question which motivates much literature on the epistemology of testimony: under what circumstances can we gain new knowledge from what other people say? This is in part because I have mostly taken up the perspective of someone attempting to be trustworthy, rather than that of someone seeking to assess others' trustworthiness. But it is also because there is no straightforward route from an account of trustworthiness to an account of testimonial knowledge-acquisition. In my view, encountering a trustworthy speaker is neither necessary or sufficient for learning something via testimony, although I will not try to vindicate that claim here.

A pragmatic disadvantage of my approach to this project is that it has obscured the ways in which my themes articulate with the work of some creative and significant philosophers who focus more specifically on injustice in the context of speech, assertion, and testimony. Yet the ideas of Miranda Fricker, Kristie Dotson, Rebecca Kukla, and their interlocutors have preoccupied me during the thinking and writing of my later chapters especially. In various ways, I have been trying to adapt and extend their insights so as to accommodate practical action more generally. So in this final section I will bring a few connections and contrasts to the surface, thereby gesturing towards an acknowledgement of these influences.

Much recent discussion of errors in trust or distrust has been framed by Fricker's very fruitful writings on epistemic injustice and the role of prejudices about social identities in generating such errors (2007). Fricker's main concern is situations in which we underestimate other people's expertise or honesty due to our systematic identity prejudices. I have mentioned a number of examples where identity prejudice and stereotyping generate obstacles to trustworthiness or, at least, obstacles to being perceived as trustworthy. But I have treated such prejudice as just one source of obstacles amongst many, and have not focused on ethical or epistemic faults as opposed to blameless use of stereotypes. In practical terms, when attempting both to be trustworthy and to maintain a reputation for trustworthiness, we need to anticipate and accommodate such reactions from others, regardless of their normative status.

For Fricker, it is important that such cases can involve distinctively epistemic harm, where someone is harmed in their capacity as a knower. There is a loose sense in which I too have been concerned with epistemic harms, since I have discussed cases in which people's knowledge and competence are unfairly underestimated, and harms are associated with that. But these have not been a special focus for me, and I have also emphasized that we can easily underestimate how difficult it is for *anyone* to be competent enough to successfully act in a given situation. This is a consequence of the decision to understand and individuate competence in such a way that, for example, getting kids to school on time in the face of major challenges requires much greater competence than getting kids to school on time when life is straightforward. When outsiders judge someone who lives in difficult circumstances, they may correctly assess her as lacking the competences she requires—but they fail to appreciate just how much competence is required to succeed against such odds.

I have argued elsewhere (Hawley 2011) that the framework of epistemic harms does not easily accommodate the reality of systematic identity-based underestimations of other people's practical competence, as opposed to their testimonial worth. Given my concern to unify treatments of the practical and testimonial spheres, I have sought to find ways of discussing phenomena related to epistemic injustice without committing to this particular framework. Compared to Fricker, I am also more concerned to retain conceptual space between being a knower and being recognized as a knower, much as I tried to retain conceptual space between being trustworthy and being regarded as trustworthy. Of course, not being taken seriously as a knower can be enormously damaging, perhaps especially when this flows from systematic prejudice. But often when we suffer from testimonial injustice one reason this is unfair is that we really do know what we are talking about.

So in various ways I depart from Fricker's theoretical framework. Despite this, the phenomena she discusses provide key examples of situations in which trustworthiness becomes difficult to manage and communicate, and in which the social stakes are high. Importantly, the accessibility, influence, and impact of Fricker's book has made it immeasurably easier to pursue this sort of project as philosophy without flagrantly violating disciplinary norms.

Kristie Dotson's rich work on types of silencing has also expanded the range of phenomena which now seem amenable to 'respectable' philosophical exploration. Moreover she demonstrates the importance of black feminists' varied discussions of testimony and of obstacles to testimonial exchange; thus she widens intellectual horizons for most of her philosophical readers. For my own purposes, Dotson's theorization of 'testimonial smothering' has been especially suggestive, although her treatment of 'testimonial quieting' is also relevant (Dotson 2011). Testimonial smothering can occur when a potential speaker decides to withhold her testimony, in anticipation of a poor audience response. More specifically, Dotson focuses on situations in which the content of what could be said is unsafe or risky, for example because it is personally or politically sensitive, or not routinely voiced by 'someone like that'. Such speech makes demands on its audience, which may or may not be competent to receive such testimony; an incompetent reception could involve puzzled misunderstanding or resentful rejection, for example. When the audience's incompetence is due to its own pernicious ignorance, and a potential speaker avoids testifying because of this, then we have a case of testimonial smothering.

Although I do not use every element of Dotson's analysis, her insights have informed my discussions of social obstacles to trustworthiness and to appearing trustworthy, and in particular the ways in which a difficult situation can generate some hard choices between the pursuit of trustworthiness and other important goals or values. Someone who faces a testimonially incompetent audience—especially where it is perniciously ignorant in Dotson's sense—knows that her attempts to make her commitment precise or else to avoid commitment altogether will likely be misconstrued, perhaps with consequences for her physical or social safety. Retreating to silence, or to polite murmurings, may be the safest option and the one most likely to be counted as trustworthy.

But silence closes off other important possibilities, including the possibility of proving one's trustworthiness to people who depend upon us; where we already have a meta-commitment to speaking out, an incompetent audience may leave us with no trustworthy course of action, since neither speaking nor remaining silent can fulfil our responsibilities. In chapter 4, I touched upon the idea that engaging in conversation generates some kind of meta-commitment to continue an exchange, to cooperate in taking on new commitments as appropriate. Where the interlocutor's testimonial incompetence becomes evident only as conversation progresses, this places the speaker in an especially difficult situation: unable easily to cut the conversation short yet unable to say what would truly be appropriate, were the audience able to receive it properly.

Finally, Kukla (2014) at one point provided the framework for an entire chapter of the present book, before I reluctantly realized, with the assistance of Heal (2013), that this did not play nicely with my overall approach. Nevertheless, the traces of Kukla's arguments and examples lie just below the surface at various points. And, like Fricker and Dotson, she demonstrates how philosophical concepts and distinctions can illuminate untidy but vitally important practical situations.

Kukla is concerned with the interplay of social power and the force of speech acts. She takes a speech act to be something which requires substantive contribution from both speaker and audience: a speaker's intentions are insufficient to determine the force of what she says, even when those intentions are recognized. Thus people sometimes try but fail to commit themselves through speech because of their social context, not least because of their social identities.

In one of Kukla's fascinating examples, a woman manager works in a male-dominated environment: she issues orders to her team using phrasing which would mark them as orders if given by a man in that context. Nevertheless, because of the unfamiliarity of female authority in this environment, the woman's utterances are heard as mere requests rather than as orders. They get relatively low compliance, which reinforces the idea that the woman lacks authority. Moreover because the woman does not see herself as merely making requests, she does not display gratitude when the workers do comply, and so they resent her for this ingratitude. There is no easy way out of this difficulty for the woman manager: if she further emphasizes that she is giving orders, she will be further resented, and if she displays gratitude, this reinforces the idea that she is merely making requests which the workers are free to grant or deny. (Recall the situation of an employer speaking to striking workers, discussed in section 6.2.)

On this picture, an audience can quash the speaker's intended force, or transform it into a different, unintended force. If I intend to assert, yet others hear me as merely questioning, then I am questioning. Moreover we can extend the picture to understand how people may end up more committed than they would like to be, rather than less committed. For example, in a committee setting, suggesting that something should be done may be treated as offering to do that thing, especially if the speaker is already regarded as being the kind of person who takes on such tasks. If such a person makes a suggestion (as she sees it) then fails to follow through with action, this will be seen as untrustworthy behaviour, because others understand her not merely to be suggesting a course of action but as committing to make it happen.

In my terms, Kukla is offering a picture according to which incurring commitment depends upon audience reaction and behaviour, so speakers often lack control over what commitments they incur. Such speakers lack control over the ways in which they become proper objects of others' trust and distrust, over what trustworthiness requires them to do. In the best-case scenario, they can detect these unwanted commitments and fulfil them, behaving as a trustworthy person does, although at some cost to themselves. But in the worst case, they either lack insight into their normative situation or lack the competence to fulfil these commitments, so are rendered untrustworthy despite their best intentions.

For better or for worse, I have held open more conceptual space between being (un)trustworthy and being regarded as (un)trustworthy, and correspondingly between incurring a commitment and being regarded as having incurred a commitment. But we can retain our grip on why Kukla's focus and examples are important, without accepting that her account of commitment-through-language is the right match for thinking about trustworthiness. We can say instead that speakers are often taken to have commitments which they do not really have, or to lack commitments which they do really have. And, depending on the circumstances, speakers either possess or lack insight into what other people take them to be committed to. A novice entering a new, difficult situation may not realize how systematically she can be misunderstood. Meanwhile, old hands may have found ways of anticipating potential misunderstandings, working around them to the extent that this is possible.

In different ways, I have approached these three authors through the conceptual connections between commitment, trustworthiness, and success in action (including truth in assertive speech). These connections inform the judgements and inferences we make about other people—accurately or inaccurately, sequentially or holistically—especially when they behave or speak in ways we find surprising. Where prejudice, pernicious ignorance, or imbalances of social power influence what we think about someone's commitment, her trustworthiness, or her action, this influence will spread to our other judgements. Moreover, we are all also on the receiving end of such judgements from other people, although some of us are more vulnerable to this than are others. Explicitly or not, we are aware of the dangers when we think about how to act, speak, and commit in the world, in situations where others will form opinions about us.

It's not easy to be trustworthy. But it can be made easier when the people around us are aware of the obstacles we encounter, and the difficult choices we face. In our turn, we can make it easier for other people to be trustworthy by taking care over the ways in which we judge their behaviour and speech.

Additional Sources

6.1 How We See Each Other. Marsh (2011) discusses our duties to trust one another, whilst Oderberg (2013) argues that we should err on the side of over-estimating others' reputations rather than underestimating them. I explore some related issues in Hawley (2014b). D'Cruz (2015) draws out the connections between trust, trustworthiness, and consistency of character. Other valuable work in this broader area includes Gambetta (2011), Jones (2012), Medina (2013), Origgi (2017), and Williams (2002).

6.2 Responding to Limited Control of Our Commitments. Sources listed for section 5.1 are relevant here.

6.3 Responding to Obstacles to Grasping Our Competence. Sources listed for section 5.2 are relevant here.

6.4 Retrospective Perspectives. Sources listed for section 5.1 are relevant here.

6.5 Testimony and Testimonials. I draw more explicit connections between trust, distrust and epistemic injustice in my (2017a). Peet (2015) provides another perspective on what can go wrong with speech, whilst both Kukla and Dotson trace links to work such as Langton (1992), Hornsby (1994), and Hornsby and Langton (1998). The papers collected within Maitra and McGowan (eds) (2012) are also significant.

References

Alston, William (2000), *Illocutionary Acts and Sentence Meaning* (Ithaca, NY: Cornell University Press).

Altham, J. E. J. (1985), 'Wicked Promises', in Ian Hacking (ed.), *Exercises in Analysis* (Cambridge: Cambridge University Press), 1–21.

Austin, J. L. (1946), 'Other Minds', *Proceedings of the Aristotelian Society* 20: 148–87.

Baier, Annette C. (1986), 'Trust and Antitrust', *Ethics* 96: 231–60.

Bird, Alexander (2002), 'Illocutionary Silencing', *Pacific Philosophical Quarterly* 83: 1–15.

Brandom, Robert (1983), 'Asserting', *Noûs* 17: 637–50.

Brown, Jessica and Cappelen, Herman (eds) (2011), *Assertion* (Oxford: Oxford University Press).

Calhoun, Cheshire (2009), 'What Good is Commitment?', *Ethics* 119: 613–41.

Cappelen, Herman (2011), 'Against Assertion', in Jessica Brown and Herman Cappelen (eds), *Assertion* (Oxford: Oxford University Press), 21–48.

Carson, Thomas L. (2010), *Lying and Deception* (New York: Oxford University Press).

Chang, Ruth (2013), 'Commitment, Reasons and the Will', in Russ Shafer-Landau (ed.), *Oxford Studies in Metaethics*, vol.8 (Oxford: Oxford University Press), 74–113.

D'Cruz, Jason (2015), 'Trust, Trustworthiness, and the Moral Consequence of Consistency', *Journal of the American Philosophical Association* 1.3: 467–84.

D'Cruz, Jason and Kalef, Justin (2015), 'Promising to Try', *Ethics* 125.3: 797–806.

Darwall, Stephen (2017), 'Trust as a Second-Personal Attitude (of the Heart)', in Paul Faulkner and Thomas Simpson (eds), *Philosophy of Trust* (Oxford: Oxford University Press), 35–50.

DeRose, Keith (2002), 'Assertion, Knowledge, and Context', *Philosophical Review* 111: 167–203.

Domenicucci, Jacopo and Holton, Richard (2017), 'Trust as a Two-Place Relation', in Paul Faulkner and Thomas Simpson (eds), *Philosophy of Trust* (Oxford: Oxford University Press), 149–60.

Dotson, Kristie (2011), 'Tracking Epistemic Violence, Tracking Practices of Silencing', *Hypatia* 26.2: 236–57.

Dougherty, Tom (2015), '*Yes Means Yes*: Consent as Communication', *Philosophy and Public Affairs* 43.3: 224–53.

Driver, Julia (1983), 'Promises, Obligations, and Abilities', *Philosophical Studies* 44: 221–3.

Driver, Julia (2011), 'Promising Too Much', in Hanoch Sheinman (ed.), *Promises and Agreements* (Oxford: Oxford University Press), 183–97.

Faulkner, Paul (2007), 'On Telling and Trusting', *Mind* 116: 875–902.

Faulkner, Paul (2015), 'The Attitude of Trust is Basic', *Analysis* 75.3: 424–9.

Faulkner, Paul (2017), 'The Problem of Trust', in Paul Faulkner and Thomas Simpson (eds), *Philosophy of Trust* (Oxford: Oxford University Press), 109–28.

Frankfurt, Harry (2005), *On Bullshit* (Princeton, NJ: Princeton University Press).

Fricker, Elizabeth (2006), 'Second-Hand Knowledge', *Philosophy and Phenomenological Research* 73.3: 592–618.

Fricker, Elizabeth (2012), 'Stating and Insinuating', *Proceedings of the Aristotelian Society Supplementary Volume* 86.1: 61–94.

Fricker, Miranda (2007), *Epistemic Injustice* (Oxford: Oxford University Press).

Gambetta, Diego (2011), *Codes of the Underworld* (Princeton, NJ: Princeton University Press).

Gettier, Edmund (1963), 'Is Justified True Belief Knowledge?', *Analysis* 23: 121–3.

Goldberg, Sanford C. (2015), *Assertion* (Oxford: Oxford University Press).

Govier, Trudy (1993), 'Self-Trust, Autonomy, and Self-Esteem', *Hypatia* 8.1: 99–120.

Grice, Paul (1989), *Studies in the Way of Words* (Cambridge, MA: Harvard University Press).

Hardin, Russell (2002), *Trust and Trustworthiness* (New York: Russell Sage Foundation).

Hardin, Russell (ed.) (2004), *Distrust* (New York: Russell Sage Foundation).

Hawley, Katherine (2003), 'Success and Knowledge-How', *American Philosophical Quarterly* 40.1: 19–31.

Hawley, Katherine (2011), 'Knowing How and Epistemic Injustice', in John Bengson and Marc A. Moffett (eds), *Knowing How* (Oxford: Oxford University Press), 283–99.

Hawley, Katherine (2012), *Trust: A Very Short Introduction* (Oxford: Oxford University Press).

Hawley, Katherine (2014a), 'Trust, Distrust and Commitment', *Noûs* 48: 1–20.

Hawley, Katherine (2014b), 'Partiality and Prejudice in Trusting', *Synthese* 191: 2029–45.

Hawley, Katherine (2017a), 'Trust, Distrust, and Epistemic Injustice', in Ian J. Kidd, José Medina, and Gaile Pohlhaus Jr (eds), *Routledge Handbook of Epistemic Injustice* (London: Routledge), 69–78.

Hawley, Katherine (2018a), 'Coercion and Lies', in Eliot Michaelson and Andreas Stokke (eds), *Lying: Language, Knowledge, Ethics, and Politics* (Oxford: Oxford University Press), 229–45.

Hawley, Katherine (2018b), 'Creativity and Knowledge', in Berys Gaut and Matthew Kieran (eds), *Creativity and Philosophy* (London: Routledge), 60–73.

Hawley, Katherine (2019), 'What Is Impostor Syndrome?', Proceedings of the Aristotelian Society Supplementary Volume 93.1: 203–26.

Hawthorne, John and Stanley, Jason (2008), 'Knowledge and Action', *Journal of Philosophy* 105.10: 571–90.

Heal, Jane (2013), 'Illocution, Recognition, and Co-operation', *Proceedings of the Aristotelian Society Supplementary Volume* 87: 137–54.

Heuer, Ulrike (2012a), 'Promising: Part 1', *Philosophy Compass* 7.12: 832–41.

Heuer, Ulrike (2012b), 'Promising: Part 2', *Philosophy Compass* 7.12: 842–51.

Hinchman, Edward S. (2005), 'Telling as Inviting to Trust', *Philosophy and Phenomenological Research* 70.3: 562–87.

Hollis, Martin (1998), *Trust Within Reason* (Cambridge: Cambridge University Press).

Holton, Richard (1994), 'Deciding to Trust, Coming to Believe', *Australasian Journal of Philosophy* 72: 63–76.

Holton, Richard (2009), *Willing, Wanting, Waiting* (Oxford: Oxford University Press).

Hornsby, Jennifer (1994), 'Illocution and its Significance', in Savas L Tsohatzidis (ed.), *Foundations of Speech Act Theory* (London: Routledge), 187–207.

Hornsby, Jennifer and Langton, Rae (1998), 'Free Speech and Illocution', *Legal Theory* 4.1: 21–37.

Intemann, Kristen (2010), '25 Years of Feminist Empiricism and Standpoint Theory: Where Are We Now?', *Hypatia* 25: 778–96.

Jones, Karen (1996), 'Trust as an Affective Attitude', *Ethics* 107: 4–25.

Jones, Karen (2002), 'The Politics of Credibility', in Louise Antony and Charlotte Witt (eds), *A Mind of One's Own: Feminist Essays on Reason and Objectivity* (2nd edn, Boulder, CO: Westview Press), 154–76.

Jones, Karen (2004), 'Trust and Terror', in Peggy DesAutels and Margaret Urban Walker (eds), *Moral Psychology* (Lanham, MD: Rowman and Littlefield), 3–18.

Jones, Karen (2012), 'Trustworthiness', *Ethics* 123.1: 61–85.

Jones, Karen (2013), 'Distrusting the Trustworthy', in David Archard, Monique Deveaux, Neil Manson, and Daniel Weinstock (eds), *Reading Onora O'Neill* (London: Routledge), 186–98.

Krishnamurthy, Meena (2015), '(White) Tyranny and the Democratic Value of Distrust', *The Monist* 94.8: 391–406.

Kukla, Rebecca (2014), 'Performative Force, Convention and Discursive Injustice', *Hypatia* 29.2: 440–57.

Lackey, Jennifer (2008), *Learning From Words* (Oxford: Oxford University Press).

Langton, Rae (1992), 'Speech Acts and Unspeakable Acts', *Philosophy and Public Affairs* 22: 293–330.

Lawlor, Krista (2013), *Assurance* (Oxford: Oxford University Press).

MacFarlane, John (2005), 'Making Sense of Relative Truth', *Proceedings of the Aristotelian Society* 105: 321–39.

MacFarlane, John (2011), 'What Is Assertion?', in Jessica Brown and Herman Cappelen (eds), *Assertion* (Oxford: Oxford University Press), 79–96.

Maitra, Ishani (2010), 'The Nature of Epistemic Injustice', *Philosophical Books* 51.4: 195–211.

Maitra, Ishani (2011), 'Assertion, Norms and Games', in Jessica Brown and Herman Cappelen (eds), *Assertion* (Oxford: Oxford University Press), 277–96.

Maitra, Ishani and McGowan, Mary Kate (eds) (2012), *Speech and Harm: Controversies Over Free Speech* (Oxford: Oxford University Press).

Marsh, Gerald (2011), 'Trust, Testimony and Prejudice in the Credibility Economy', *Hypatia* 26.2: 280–93.

Marušić, Berislav (2013), 'Promising Against the Evidence', *Ethics* 123.2: 292–317.

Marušić, Berislav (2015), *Evidence and Agency* (Oxford: Oxford University Press).

McLeod, Carolyn (2002), *Self-Trust and Reproductive Autonomy* (Cambridge, MA: MIT Press).

McLeod, Carolyn (2015), 'Trust', in Edward N. Zalta (ed.), *Stanford Encyclopedia of Philosophy* (Fall 2015 Edition), https://plato.stanford.edu/archives/fall2015/entries/trust/.

Medina, José (2013), *The Epistemology of Resistance: Gender and Racial Oppression, Epistemic Injustice, and Resistant Imaginations* (Oxford: Oxford University Press).

Mills, Charles W. (2007), 'White Ignorance', in Shannon Sullivan and Nancy Tuana (eds), *Race and Epistemologies of Ignorance* (Albany, NY: State University of New York Press), 11–38.

Moran, Richard (2005), 'Getting Told and Being Believed', *Philosophers Imprint* 5.5: 1–29.

Nickel, Philip J. (2007), 'Trust and Obligation-Ascription', *Journal of Ethical Theory and Moral Practice* 10: 309–19.

Oderberg, David (2013), 'The Morality of Reputation and the Judgement of Others', *Journal of Practical Ethics* 1.2: 3–33.

O'Neill, Onora (2002a), *Autonomy and Trust in Bioethics* (Cambridge: Cambridge University Press).

O'Neill, Onora (2002b), *A Question of Trust* (Cambridge: Cambridge University Press).

Origgi, Gloria (2017), *Reputation* (Princeton, NJ: Princeton University Press).

Owens, David (2006), 'Testimony and Assertion', *Philosophical Studies* 130.1: 105–29.

Owens, David (2012), *Shaping the Normative Landscape* (Oxford: Oxford University Press).

Peet, Andrew (2015), 'Epistemic Injustice in Utterance Interpretation', *Synthese* 194.9: 3421–43.

Peirce, C. S. (1932), *Collected Papers of Charles Sanders Peirce*, vol 2, ed. C. Hartshorne and P. Weiss (Cambridge, MA: Harvard University Press).

Potter, Nancy Nyquist (2002), *How Can I Be Trusted?* (Lanham, MD: Rowan and Littlefield).

Putnam, Robert D. (2000), *Bowling Alone: The Collapse and Revival of American Community* (New York: Simon and Schuster).

Ratcliffe, Matthew, Ruddell, Mark, and Smith, Benedict (2014), 'What is a Sense of 'Foreshortened Future'? A Phenomenological Study of Trauma, Trust and Time', *Frontiers in Psychology* 5: article 1026.

Rawls, John (1971), *A Theory of Justice* (Cambridge, MA: Harvard University Press).

Rescorla, Michael (2009), 'Assertion and its Constitutive Norms', *Philosophy and Phenomenological Research* 79: 98–130.

Sakulku, Jaruwan and Alexander, James (2011), 'The Impostor Phenomenon', *International Journal of Behavioral Science* 6.1: 73–92.

Sarsons, Heather and Xu, Guo (2015), 'Confidence Men? Gender and Confidence: Evidence Among Top Economists', working paper, https://scholar.harvard.edu/files/sarsons/files/confidence_final.pdf/.

Saul, Jennifer (2012), *Lying, Misleading, and What Is Said* (Oxford: Oxford University Press).

Scanlon, T. M. (1998), *What We Owe to Each Other* (Cambridge, MA: Harvard University Press).

Searle, John (1969), *Speech Acts: An Essay in the Philosophy of Language* (Cambridge: Cambridge University Press).

Sheinman, Hanoch (ed.) (2011), *Promises and Agreements* (Oxford: Oxford University Press).

Shiffrin, Seana (2014), *Speech Matters* (Princeton, NJ: Princeton University Press).

Simon, Judith (2013), 'Trust', *Oxford Bibliographies in Philosophy*, http://www.oxfordbibliographies.com/view/document/obo-9780195396577/obo-97801953 96577-0157.xml.

Smith, Holly M. (1997), 'A Paradox of Promising', *Philosophical Review* 106.2: 153–96.

Sosa, Ernest (2010), 'How Competence Matters in Epistemology', *Philosophical Perspectives*, 24.1: 465–75.

Srinivasan, Amia (2015), 'Normativity without Cartesian Privilege', *Philosophical Issues* 25.1: 273–99.

Stokke, Andreas (2014), 'Insincerity', *Noûs* 48.3: 496–520.

Stoljar, Natalie (2013), 'Feminist Perspectives on Autonomy', in Edward N. Zalta (ed.), *Stanford Encyclopedia of Philosophy* (Fall 2015 Edition), https://plato.stanford.edu/archives/fall2015/entries/feminism-autonomy/.

Strawson, P. F. (1974), 'Freedom and Resentment', in *Freedom and Resentment* (London: Methuen), 1–25.

Sunstein, Cass (2007), 'Moral Heuristics and Risk', in Tim Lewens (ed.), *Risk: Philosophical Perspectives* (London: Routledge), 156–70.

Thompson, Christopher (2017), 'Trust Without Reliance', *Ethical Theory and Moral Practice* 20.3: 643–55.

Thomson, Judith Jarvis (1990), *The Realm of Rights* (Cambridge, MA: Harvard University Press).

Watson, Gary (2004), 'Asserting and Promising', *Philosophical Studies* 117.1–2: 57–77.

Weiner, Matthew (2005), 'Must We Know What We Say?', *Philosophical Review* 114.2: 227–51.

White, Roger (2005), 'Epistemic Permissiveness', *Philosophical Perspectives* 19: 445–59.

Williams, Bernard (2002), *Truth and Truthfulness* (Princeton, NJ: Princeton University Press).

Williamson, Timothy (1996), 'Knowing and Asserting', *Philosophical Review* 105: 489–523.

Williamson, Timothy (2000), *Knowledge and its Limits* (Oxford: Oxford University Press).

Zagzebski, Linda (1996), *Virtues of the Mind* (Cambridge: Cambridge University Press).

Zimmerman, Michael (2014), *Ignorance and Moral Responsibility* (Oxford: Oxford University Press).

Index

"neologism?"